AZUSA STREET B(

CECIL M.

AND

DARRIN RODGERS

How Pentecost Came to Los Angeles

The Story behind the Azusa Street Revival

~

FRANK BARTLEMAN

GPH®
Gospel Publishing House
02-4226

Originally published as
How Pentecost Came to Los Angeles:
As It Was in the Beginning.
Frank Bartleman, Los Angeles, 1925

This book is unabridged and unedited
from a copy of the original print run.

Series Foreword and Introduction © 2017 by Gospel Publishing House, 1445 N. Boonville Ave., Springfield, Missouri 65802. All rights reserved. No part of this book may be reproduced, stored in a retrieval system, or transmitted in any form or by any means— electronic, mechanical, photocopy, recording, or otherwise—without prior written permission of the publisher, except brief quotations used in connection with reviews in magazines or newspapers.

ISBN: 978-1-60731-491-2

19 18 17 • 1 2 3

Printed in United States of America

CONTENTS

This little book is dedicated to the many precious souls who with the author were privileged to see and experience the early days of blessing of the "Latter Rain" outpouring at the old "power-house," Azusa Street Mission. It is written with the hope and prayer that, where lost, the vision may be renewed to those who once shared with us in the glory of this "former house" of blessing; and also that it may, through this humble little medium, be told "to the generation following."

Frank Bartleman
Los Angeles, California
April 1925

Series Foreword

Cecil M. Robeck Jr.

Over a century has passed since the Azusa Street Revival (1906–1909), the remarkable spiritual outpouring in Los Angeles that became a focal point of the emerging Pentecostal Movement. Pentecostals/charismatics, sometimes described as "Renewalists" these days, have exploded in growth in recent years, and now include as many as 670 million people worldwide. They are not all identified as Classical Pentecostals, but they have embraced the experience of baptism in the Holy Spirit and manifest the gifts or charisms of the Holy Spirit in very similar ways. With this growth has come renewed interest in the faith and testimonies of early Pentecostals, including those at the Azusa Street Revival.

This volume is part of the Azusa Street Series, which once again brings into print several of the earliest published accounts of the Azusa Street Revival and its fruit. These primary resources, which provide context and tell the story of the revival, were originally published primarily for popular audiences. However, they have since proven to be of importance for those within the academic world who wish to understand this singularly significant revival for the ongoing life of the Church today.

It is my hope that in reading these volumes, you will be challenged in new or refreshing ways by what God has to offer to you. Sister Aimee Semple McPherson, pastor of Angelus Temple in Los Angeles and founder of the International Church of the Foursquare Gospel, quoted the writer of Hebrews (13:8) who wrote so profoundly, "Jesus Christ [is] the same, yesterday, to day, and for ever!" She required that text to be displayed in or on every Foursquare church building. This message—that God is unchanging and that the vibrant spiritual life of the early Church is still available today—was an essential part of the preaching of the apostle Peter when he said that "the promise is unto you, and to your children, and to all that are afar off, even as many as the Lord our God shall call" (Acts 2:39), and it quickly became part of the worldview embraced by early Pentecostals. May the volumes in this series, likewise, continue to remind Pentecostals of their spiritual heritage and identity.

Introduction

The Azusa Street Revival and Its Early Impact

Cecil M. Robeck Jr.

The revival that took place at the Azusa Street Mission in Los Angeles, California at the beginning of the twentieth century is without parallel in the story of the Pentecostal Movement. It began in 1906, shortly after an African American pastor, William J. Seymour, arrived in Los Angeles where he had been invited to become the pastor of a small Holiness congregation. He had traveled from Houston, Texas, arriving in Los Angeles on February 22. While in Houston, Pastor Seymour had been a student at Charles Parham's Apostolic Faith Bible School for about six weeks.

Shortly after Seymour began his ministry with that little storefront congregation, part of the Holiness Church of Southern California and Arizona, he preached a sermon that was based upon the experience of those who waited in Jerusalem as Jesus had commanded them, and were subsequently baptized in the Holy Spirit (Acts 1:4, 8 and 2:4). He explained to his flock that this was the pattern of empowerment intended for the whole church, and as such, his congregation could ask and expect to be baptized in the Holy Spirit in the very same way and with the very same evidence, the "Bible evidence," that is, the ability to speak in other tongues. Some members of the congregation were open to his message, but others were not. A meeting with denominational leaders was called to evaluate his theology, and by the following week, Pastor Seymour found himself without a job.

Fortunately, one of the African American couples, Edward and Mattie Lee, who were part of this congregation, invited Pastor Seymour to stay with them while he sought the mind of the Lord on what to do next. During the evenings they shared together, Brother Seymour led them in prayer and Bible study. He continued to share with them his conviction that if they sought the Lord, He would baptize them in the Holy Spirit just as He had done for those who waited for the Promise of the Father in Jerusalem. As their relationship developed, the Lees invited other friends to join them in hearing William Seymour. This was where Frank Bartleman, the primary chronicler of the Azusa Street Revival, first met Pastor Seymour. At the same time, Pastor Seymour sent for a couple of friends from Houston to join him. One of them was another African American, Mrs. Lucy Farrow, who had been baptized in the Holy Spirit under the ministry of Charles Parham. She would become a great helper to Seymour in the days that followed. As the meeting outgrew the Lee home, it moved to the home of another African American couple, Richard and Ruth Asberry, at 214 North Bonnie Brae Street.

On April 9, 1906, Edward Lee came home from his janitorial job, complaining that he didn't feel well. He asked Seymour to pray for him so that they could attend the prayer meeting at the Asberry home. Pastor Seymour laid hands on Edward Lee and prayed for his healing, and then Lucy Farrow joined him

Nazarene congregation, when they were baptized in the Holy Spirit.

Within eight months of its first service, the Azusa Street Mission had been joined by Elmer K. Fisher, who led a congregation that resulted from a split in Joseph Smale's First New Testament Church. It took the name, Upper Room Mission. Thomas G. Atteberry began holding Pentecostal meetings at the People's Church, while the Holiness Church in Sawtelle, west of downtown Los Angeles, would form yet another Pentecostal congregation, this one led by young women from First New Testament Church and the Azusa Street Mission. Finally, Charles F. Parham began to hold meetings in Los Angeles in November 1906. His was the only work that intentionally attempted to counter or compete with the work of the Azusa Street Mission. He did so, arguing that Seymour's work was a complete distortion of anything he had tried to teach Seymour when Seymour was one of his students.

From 1900 to 1907, Parham had been the most recognizable Pentecostal in the United States. He had been reared in the Methodist Church, and for a period of time, he served as a Methodist pastor. During those years, however, he came to embrace a series of beliefs that led him to form what he called the Apostolic Faith Movement. He believed in and established several short-term Bible schools in Topeka, Kansas; Houston, Texas; and Baxter Springs, Kansas. There he taught students about the need for evangelism; he emphasized living lives of holiness, prayer for the healing of the sick, and from late 1900s, baptism in the Holy Spirit with the "Bible evidence" of speaking in tongues. These tongues, he claimed, were not foreign languages that people had learned, but rather foreign languages that were spontaneous gifts or charisms of the Holy Spirit that they had not learned, but that they could now use to evangelize the nations.

While Parham taught these things, which became hallmarks of early Pentecostal theology, he also accepted some teachings that have never been accepted in Christian or Pentecostal orthodoxy. Through the influence of his wife's family, he embraced a theory of British Israelitism, the idea that when the tribes of Israel returned to Palestine from Babylon, some tribes remained in Babylon and were ultimately lost to history. They became the British people. Even before 1900, he joined the Zionist Movement of Jews that was advocating a return to Israel as their God-given homeland. Pressure for such a Zionist land for Jews alone contributed to the current troubles between Israel and the Palestinians today. He argued also that only those who had been baptized in the Holy Spirit would ultimately be raptured when Christ returns, and in some measure, he seems to have argued that those with an African heritage would not be part of that rapture. Furthermore, he maintained that the wicked would ultimately be annihilated, thereby denying the existence of hell.

William J. Seymour had enrolled in Charles Parham's Houston Bible school in January 1906. Texas was a racially segregated state at that time, unwilling to allow African Americans and Caucasians to be educated in the same schools or classrooms. Parham decided to follow the letter of the law, but not its spirit, when he allowed Seymour to have access to his lectures. He moved Seymour's seat outside the classroom by an open door, so that Seymour could hear. There it was that William Seymour learned of the baptism in the Spirit and he began a quest of several months to receive it. He did not give up tarrying for it, even though he had not yet received it when he arrived in Los Angeles. He finally received the baptism in the Holy Spirit after a number of those that he was teaching and with whom he was praying received it before him. When he finally received the Baptism and spoke in other tongues, he led his Azusa Street congregation with wisdom, even though his services could be labeled as somewhat experimental.

What I mean by calling them experimental is that apart from Charles Parham and his small Apostolic Faith Movement in Kansas, Missouri, and Texas, there were few who had any real idea about how a Pentecostal service was to be conducted or what Pentecostals believed. William Seymour clearly accepted parts of Parham's teachings, but he rejected other parts, for instance, his British Israelite teaching and his theory regarding the ultimate annihilation of the wicked. But instead of relying on someone else's theological system, Seymour decided that the Bible would be the sole focus for shedding light upon how the congregation would function and what the congregation believed, though ultimately, he held to the Articles of Faith that had been taught by John Wesley in the Methodist Church.

The fact that seating in the Azusa Street Mission was arranged in a circle, with Pastor Seymour in the center of the room, meant that people faced one another. They could see one another and could speak to one another, face-to-face. They sang, they prayed, they preached, they testified, they prophesied and spoke in tongues, and they argued. Yes, they argued! They argued about those things especially that seemed to set them off in distinctive ways from other congregations and denominations. They argued over how to interpret various biblical passages. They disagreed about what constituted divine expectations regarding personal holiness. They argued over the limits of orderly conduct in a Pentecostal meeting, what was acceptable and what was not. They disputed with one another over the number and nature of spiritual gifts, and whether tongues was the "Bible evidence" of their baptism in the Spirit as was suggested in Acts 2, or intended to be understood solely as a charism or gift of the Holy Spirit as is outlined in 1 Corinthians 12–14. Slowly, their arguments led to a consensus that yielded a commitment to what we now know as Pentecostal doctrine and Pentecostal order.

While William Seymour was clearly the acknowledged pastor and leader of the Azusa Street Mission, and he performed all of the functions that pastors typically perform, there were many services in which he functioned much more as a facilitator, allowing the service to progress as different people offered "a hymn, a word of instruction, a revelation, a tongue, or an interpretation" (1 Corinthians 14:26). While we have only fragments or summaries of a few of the sermons that Pastor Seymour offered to his congregation, we have a number of reports that describe the ways in which the various services ran. They began with prayer, often on their knees and they prayed in silence, sometimes for very long periods, in a kind of "holy hush," as the Holy Spirit moved among them. They sang many of the revival songs that were popular in camp meetings and especially in Methodist and Holiness churches. On many occasions, they sang in tongues, a phenomenon that impressed even the members of the secular press with its character that they acknowledged demanded "awe" for the One who had sent it. Something new, something special was happening at those times. And then there were the periods of personal testimony, at times lasting upwards of three hours, as people lined up to tell others of their latest or freshest experience of the Holy Spirit, or their most recent answer to prayer, or simply to express their newly found joy in the Lord. There were the debates, of course, but there was also preaching, and the floor was open to men and women alike. Pastor Seymour freely allowed others to "fill the pulpit," trusting the Holy Spirit and the people of God to recognize what the Lord wanted them to know.

Charles Parham would later write that when William Seymour was a student of his, he would take Seymour one-on-one into the African American community, where Seymour would preach. He believed that Seymour held considerable leadership potential, and with his primary associate, Warren Faye Carothers, Parham even considered the possibility that Seymour might be put in charge of the "colored section" in his racially segregated Apostolic Faith Movement in Texas. When Seymour chose to leave Houston and accept the call to lead the nameless Holiness congregation in Los Angeles, Parham had been disappointed. In the ensuing months from February through August, Parham more and more came to terms with Seymour's decision and the idea that Seymour represented him and his Apostolic Faith interests on the West Coast. It appears that Seymour agreed with this idea, for during this period he sent several letters to Parham and to W. F. Carothers, requesting his preaching credential in the Apostolic Faith Movement, asking for buttons that his own members could wear that would identify them also as members of the Apostolic Faith Movement, and these items were sent to him. He also accepted into his inner circle several people that Parham sent to Los Angeles, in order to get firsthand reports from those he trusted regarding the success of Seymour's work. All of them reported favorably. Seymour also announced repeatedly in the Apostolic Faith newspaper published by the Azusa Street Mission, how much he appreciated Charles Parham. Finally, once Parham arrived in Los Angeles,

Seymour gave him a seat of honor, and introduced Parham as his "father in the faith." Why, then, did Charles Parham turn against William J. Seymour and the revival that brought thousands of people to the Azusa Street Mission where they were saved, healed, baptized in the Spirit, and sent out as evangelists and missionaries?

As I have worked my way through the many writings of Charles Parham, it seems clear that the most significant frustrations he had with Seymour and the work at Azusa Street had to do with the differences of culture and style. Charles Parham was white; William Seymour was black. Neither Missouri nor Kansas was considered to be a Southern state in which slavery had been supported, yet both became entangled in the Civil War, with citizens on both sides of that issue. Texas, however, was a Southern state and Parham's primary associate, W. F. Carothers, was an ardent segregationist. Parham had been ministering for some time in Texas, where the segregation of the races was the law. On the other hand, California had been admitted to the United States as a "free" state, with slavery banned from its territory. And Los Angeles had a history of African Americans holding public office, living in racially integrated neighborhoods, attending racially integrated schools and churches, and benefiting from considerable racial mixing in everyday life.

When Parham came to the Azusa Street Mission, he preached two or three times by his own recollection, but he apparently exploded when he chose in his last sermon at the Mission to declare that "God is sick to His stomach" with what Parham had found there. Parham believed that one of the leaders upon whom Seymour relied, Glenn Cook, was too fanatical to be given any position within the Mission. He had come from the Burning Bush congregation, a group long known for their acerbic attitude towards anyone who differed with them. Yet Seymour had found Cook useful and made him the Mission's business manager. Parham accused Seymour of using "over-zealous" and "ignorant" workers who tried too hard to help people receive the baptism in the Holy Spirit. As a result, he labeled much of what he observed to be fake, not genuine manifestations of the Holy Spirit. He went on to complain that appropriate rules that would separate women from men and segregate the races, especially at the altar, were not in place, resulting in a breakdown of what he considered to be proper decorum. He argued that this lack of rules contributed to sexual immorality, something of which he accused the Mission, but for which there is no evidence. He also complained loudly that the style of worship at the Mission was too black and too fanatical. White folks were now imitating black folk and claiming that it was the Holy Spirit at work in them. Clearly, the mixing of races was a major issue that Parham rejected by claiming that it was God who was sickened by what Seymour allowed. These observations gave way to Parham's decision to label Seymour as an incompetent and duplicitous leader, and the many who Seymour had commissioned as pastors, evangelists, and the more than twenty he had sent out as missionaries, as unfit for ministry!

Needless to say, many of Azusa Street's workers and members were deeply offended by Parham's quick and biased, even racist, assessment of the situation. Everything that had occurred prior to Parham's arrival in Los Angeles had been done in the presence of Parham's own scouts, who had written glowing reports of the work to Charles Parham. While Seymour believed and taught that the culturally based class, racial, and ethnic distinctions embraced by much of American society were not consistent with what the Bible taught, Parham seems to have suggested that it was precisely these types of regulations that needed to be enforced at the Mission if the revival were to be genuine. Frank Bartleman summed up his disgust when he complained, "Why should [he] claim authority over us? We had prayed down our own revival."

Charles Parham obviously did not understand the differences that existed between what he found in the South and what he might have seen in Los Angeles had he spent more time in the city. Los Angeles was filled with a broad range of racial and ethnic groups, many of whom were brand-new immigrants to the United States at the time. There were significant colonies, communities, or ghettos within the city, filled with a multitude of languages, among them Russian, Armenian, Danish, Swedish, Norwegian, Italian, German, Spanish, Japanese, Chinese, and Hebrew, just to name a few. Most of these new immigrants and refugees did not yet have adequate facility with the English language at the time. In fact, a secular group known as the "Liberal Alliance" worked with these immigrants, hoping to make them better citizens by explaining and interpreting the US Constitution and their rights under that constitution, and offering courses in English. Still, many of these people continued to live within their linguistically limited colonies. As a result, within a decade, one could find Swedish, Armenian, Russian, Italian, and several Spanish language congregations that were a direct outgrowth of the Azusa Street Mission. Their intent was not competition, but cooperation across language barriers.

Over the next several years, the influence of the Azusa Street Revival could be felt in many places throughout the United States and around the world. The impact of this revival continues to extend even to the present. When Gaston

Barnabas Cashwell (or GB as he was more popularly known) traveled from North Carolina to Los Angeles to seek his baptism in the Holy Spirit and then returned to preach the message of "Pentecost" to representatives from a variety of Holiness churches and associations, it ultimately led to the move of a number of churches into the Pentecostal fold—many Free Will Baptists formed the Pentecostal Free Will Baptist Church, the Fire-Baptized Holiness Church became a Pentecostal body as well. It was one of the predecessors to the International Pentecostal Holiness Church, which received the message and moved into the Pentecostal camp by 1907. Early in 1907, Bishop Charles H. Mason traveled to Los Angeles, where he was baptized in the Spirit. He helped move the Church of God in Christ from the Holiness camp to become a Pentecostal denomination. The following year, Ambrose J. Tomlinson, General Overseer of the Church of God (Cleveland, Tennessee), invited Cashwell to speak at the group's annual assembly. Bishop Tomlinson was baptized in the Holy Spirit, and the denomination joined the growing Pentecostal Movement.

There were many who went out from Azusa Street to begin their own denominations. In 1908, Florence Crawford, who had originally been appointed to help establish Apostolic Faith Missions along the West Coast on behalf of the Los Angeles work under Pastor Seymour, decided to take those missions and establish her own Pentecostal work, with her headquarters in Portland, Oregon. It became known as The Apostolic Faith Movement (Portland, Oregon). The very controversial African American preacher, Henry Prentiss (sometimes spelled Prentice) ultimately traveled to Indianapolis where he played a formative role in the establishment of the Pentecostal Assemblies of the World in that city, largely through the testimony that he brought to G. T. Haywood, who would become the leading bishop of that Oneness Pentecostal organization. Thomas Hezmahalch would leave Azusa Street and, accompanied by John G. Lake, would meet in Indianapolis and travel to South Africa, where they established the Apostolic Faith Mission of South Africa. Romanita Carbajal de Valenzuela played the formative role in establishing La Iglesia Apostólica de la Fe in Cristo Jesús, the oldest and largest Pentecostal body in Mexico.

While Thomas Ball Barratt, the pastor of a Methodist congregation in Oslo, Norway, visited the United States on a fund-raising mission, he stayed at the Alliance House in New York City where he ran across a copy of Azusa Street's *Apostolic Faith*. The articles he read piqued his interest in receiving the baptism in the Holy Spirit. As a result, he began corresponding with the mission. In December 1906, several new missionaries traveling from Azusa Street to various points in Africa and the Middle East also stayed at the Alliance House. It was there, through the encouragement and prayer of Mrs. Lucy Leatherman, that Barratt was baptized in the Spirit. He traveled first to England, and then moved quickly on to Norway where he began a Pentecostal ministry that brought many church leaders from a variety of denominations into the Pentecostal fold, not only in Norway, but throughout Scandinavia, northwestern Europe (Belgium, the Netherlands, France, and Germany, etc.) and England. Through the German Pentecostals, the movement spread southward into Switzerland and eastward into Poland, the Baltic States, and Russia. Frank Bartleman ministered in a number of these countries and ministered as far east as St. Petersburg, Russia.

In 1907, William Durham, a Baptist pastor in Chicago, traveled to Los Angeles where he was baptized in the Holy Spirit

sent out from the Mission—that contributed ultimately to the formation of the Assemblies of God in Hot Springs, Arkansas, April 2–12, 1914. The Assemblies of God began on the eighth anniversary of the outpouring of the Holy Spirit on William J. Seymour's small prayer and Bible study as it met in the Asberry home on North Bonnie Brae Street in Los Angeles, the beginning of the Azusa Street Revival.

From this very brief survey of the Azusa Street Mission and the revival that ran around the clock from April 1906 until 1909, it is easy to see that its impact was enormous. No other Pentecostal congregation has had a similar impact upon the Christian Church, as its influence moved from Los Angeles, across North America, into Europe, Latin America, Africa, and Asia.

CHAPTER 1

~~

Trials and Blessings.
Revival Begins

The author of the following pages arrived in Los Angeles, Calif., with wife and two daughters, the oldest three and one-half years old, Dec. 22, 1904, after two years' mission work in the north, having crossed the continent previously, by easy stages. (See, "From Plough to Pulpit," price 50c, for previous experiences.)

After stopping one night at Peniel Mission, 227 S. Main St., we rented two unfurnished rooms, upstairs, without heat, of friends at 1055 Temple St. I had little money. I secured some furniture, and we cooked and ate under a tent in the yard. Being cold and rainy, we suffered much. Our youngest child became sick, but God spared her. The harvest was great but the laborers few in those days; there was plenty of mission work all around us, but the question was how were our needs to be supplied.

I started a street meeting, but an officer promptly stopped me. I had no permit, so went to work with the regular missions. Every night found me taking part in services, and my days were spent in personal work. We lived by faith, having no income. I had served the Lord largely on that line since my conversion in 1893, having been called to preach soon after. Wife was one with me.

Dec. 31, we had received but 50 cents since coming to Los Angeles. We were stranded. My health had been poor, from a child. I wrote in my diary at that time: My health is quite poor, but I believe I shall live to finish my work. Few care to go into the hard places, but my work is to go where others will not go. It seems God can only get a man who has nothing but Heaven to live for to do the work for which a strong man is needed. I am glad to be used up in His service. I would rather wear out than rust out; and rather starve for God, if need be, than fatten for the devil." That was about the spirit of my consecration.

January 2, I testified and helped in an all-day meeting at Boyle Heights M. E. Church, walking there, not having car-fare. Being very tired I asked the Lord for my car-fare home, and found a nickel on the side-walk. I rode home.

I preached at Fifth Street Mission, where the "Burning Bush" had gotten control. God preciously anointed me as I exhorted to a middle-ground between formalism and fanaticism. They were going wild. Jesus was crucified "between two thieves." The devil splits a work in the middle, runs away with the heart, leaving the shell, thus driving the saints to both extremes, and destroys the whole. We are creatures of extremes.

Little Esther, our oldest child, was seized with convulsions, and passed away to be with Jesus January 7, at 4 A.M. She had been a great sufferer all her life, being very frail from birth. This time it seemed God's will to take her. I was constrained to pray that she might be spared from so much suffering. I felt I was holding her by my prayers and prolonging her suffering. God wanted her but would not tear her from me. He made me willing to give her up, and then he took her. She soon passed

We had powerful meetings, with wonderful altar services. The Spirit wrought mightily. February 6, I brought wife and little Ruth to Pasadena, to the mission home. The fight was on. An enemy tried to persuade the Fergusons in Los Angeles to stop the meetings. But God put him to bed with the grippe. I determined not to eat or sleep again until victory came, so I fasted and prayed all one day. That night the Lord broke forth in power. He could not afford to have me die on His hands. I could not preach for the presence of God. The glory played on my face like a hot sun bath. God spoke that night. The altar was full until after midnight with earnest seekers.

My work here seemed finished for the time, so I rented two unfurnished rooms at 213 Grove Street, Pasadena for five dollars per month, and moved my family there, bringing our furniture from Los Angeles. I was very tired and worn in body. My nerves had been worn threadbare from years of previous pioneer mission work in various parts of the country. We had always worked on faith lines, having taken for our motto Isa. 33-16-"Bread shall be given him; his waters shall be sure." We had no money and so it seemed necessary for me to find employment for a season. At that time I had not yet turned my back fully on secular employment, as He led me so clearly to do later, although I had already been preaching for more than ten years.

While souls had been saved during the month's meetings in Peniel Mission, yet the greatest victory gained was the digging out of a company of young men attending there. A number were called out by the Lord for future service. Principal among these were Edward Boehmer, Amil Allen and Orville Tingle. Two of these at least have become very active in the Pentecostal work of today. Sister Mamie Craybill took an active part also in these meetings, especially in the ministry of intercession.

She was a very choice vessel of the Lord, later becoming active in the Pentecostal work also.

In much weakness of body I secured work gardening. This provided us with food. I preached frequently on the streets, and helped in the mission. My next job was picking oranges, from a ladder, but I had to quit at noon the first day. The weight of the fruit and the twisting on the ladder nearly broke my back. That was my weak spot. I got more gardening, and fence building. This was not so hard. Almost every night found me in some meeting, preaching or testifying. It was my life. My first call was to preach.

We suffered much from the cold and rain as we had only a little gas burner in the house, both for heating and cooking. Little Ruth was taken sick with fever, and we were about out of food. Work was scarce. I preached at Peniel Mission, without mentioning our need, but declared my faith in God to stand by the man who would stand by Him. They prayed for Ruth's healing and the Lord touched her at home while we prayed. A brother handed me five dollars after the service. Thus God had stood by me.

I distributed many tracts in Los Angeles, among the harlots and the saloons. My spare time was all spent in tract and personal work, or preaching on the street and in the missions. I only rested when I slept, and then I was often praying. I was greatly burdened for souls. "There is none that stirreth up himself to take hold of Thee." (Isa. 64:7.)

Brother Allen, one of the mission boys, gave me work painting. He was a contractor. I worked for some time at this. One day the devil tried to kill me. I was painting the gable end of a barn, from a ladder, which stood on a slanting shed roof. Suddenly, without warning, the ladder slipped and fell.

But I landed squarely on my feet on the roof, well balanced. It was done too quickly to realize it. My paint spilled all over the roof. Ps. 91:11, 12, immediately came to me. The angels of the Lord had "borne me up." I could have rolled off the roof and broken my neck.

April 8, I heard F. B. Myer, from London, preach. He described the great revival then going on in Wales, which he had just visited. He had met Evan Roberts. My soul was stirred to its depths, having read of this revival shortly before. I then and there promised God He should have full right of way with me, if He could use me.

Mother Wheaton, the prison evangelist, came to Pasadena and preached in Peniel. She was on fire for God. I longed to be wholly engaged in the work of the Lord once more but knew not how my family should be supported. The obstacles seemed very great, and my strength small. But the call of God was upon me. My family belonged to Him. If He called me I dared not fail.

I distributed tracts in the post office, banks, and public buildings in Los Angeles, and also visited many saloons with tracts. Later I visited about thirty saloons in Los Angeles again. The houses of prostitution were wide open at that time and I gave out many tracts there.

Little Esther's death had broken my heart and I felt I could only live while in God's service. I longed to know Him in a more real way and to see the work of God go forth in power. A great burden and cry came in my heart for a mighty revival. He was preparing me for a fresh service for Him. This could only be brought about by the realization of a deeper need in my own heart for God, and a real soul travail for the work of God. This He gave me. Many were being similarly prepared at this time in different parts of the world. The Lord was preparing to visit and deliver his people once more. Intercessors were the need. "He wondered that there was no intercessor." —Isa. 59:16. "I sought for a man to stand in the gap before me for the land, that I should not destroy it; but I found none." —Ezek. 22:30.

About the first of May a powerful revival broke out in the Lake Avenue M. E. Church in Pasadena. The young men who had been dug out in the meetings in Peniel Mission most of them attended this church. They had gotten under the burden for a revival there. In fact we had been praying for a sweeping revival for Pasadena. God was answering our prayers. I found a wonderful work of the Spirit going on at Lake Avenue. The altar was full of seeking souls. There was no big preacher there. One night nearly every unsaved soul in the house got saved. It was a clean sweep for God. Conviction was mightily upon the people. In two weeks' time two hundred souls knelt at the altar, seeking the Lord. The Peniel boys were underneath, and wonderfully used of God. We then began to pray for an out-pouring of the Spirit for Los Angeles and the whole of Southern California.

I find the following observations in my diary, written at that time: "Some Holiness churches (foremost at that time) are going to be surprised to find God passing them by. He will work in channels where they will yield to him. They must humble themselves for Him to come. We are crying, 'Pasadena for God!' The people are too well satisfied with their own goodness. They have little faith or interest for the salvation of others. God will humble them by passing them by. The Spirit is breathing prayer through us for a mighty, general outpouring. Great things are coming. We are asking largely, that our joy may be full. God is moving. We are praying for the churches and their pastors. The Lord will visit those willing to yield to Him."

And the same is true today of the Pentecostal people. Their ultimate failure or success for God will be realized just at this point. We must keep humble and little in our own eyes. Let us get built up by a sense of our own importance and we are gone. History repeats itself in this connection. God has always sought a humble people. He can use no other. Martin Luther, the great reformer, wrote: "When our Lord and Master Jesus Christ says repent, he means that the whole life of believers on earth should be a constant and perpetual repentance. Repentance and sorrow—i.e. true repentance—endure as long as a man is displeased with himself—that is, until he passes from this life into eternity. The desire of self-justification is the cause of all the distresses of the heart." There is much need always of heart preparation, in humility and separation, before God can consistently come. **The depth of any revival will be determined exactly by the spirit of repentance that obtains.** In fact this is the key to every true revival born of God.

May 12, God dealt with me about giving all my time to Him, turning my back finally and for all time on secular employment. He wanted me now to trust Him fully for myself and family. I had just received a little book, "The Great Revival in Wales," written by S. B. Shaw. Taking a little walk before breakfast I was reading this. The Lord had been trying for years to bring me to this decision for his service. We entered into a new contract between us. He was to have the rest of my life fully. And I have never dared to break this contract. I love work, and have been terribly tempted at times, through seeming need. I have always worked harder than my natural strength reasonably allowed.

Wife kept my breakfast for me. But I did not return until noon. I had lost my appetite for food. The Spirit, through the little book, set me on fire. I visited and prayed with three preachers and a number of workers before I returned home, at noon. I had received a new commission and anointing. My burden was for a revival. A brother gave me the money for a new pair of shoes I needed. Thus already the Lord was providing. The devil was tempting me about my contract. I had had no work for three weeks. God had closed the door to work against me.

I visited and prayed with people all day long for some time now, distributing G. Campbell Morgan's pamphlet on the "Revival in Wales." It moved the people strongly. The spirit of prayer was increasing upon me and I determined to be "obedient to the heavenly vision." The "bread question" had faced me down for many years. I prayed the Lord for faith to trust Him fully. "Man shall not live by bread alone." —Matt. 4:4.

The Lord blessed me with a further spirit of exhortation to revival among the churches, giving me articles to write for the Holiness press along the same line also. I began to write particularly for the "Way of Faith" and "God's Revivalist." One night I awoke from my sleep shouting the praises of God. He was getting hold of me more and more. I was now going day and night, exhorting to faith in God for mighty things. The spirit of revival consumed me. The spirit of prophecy came upon me strongly, also. I seemed to receive a definite "gift of faith" for revival. We were evidently in the beginning of wonderful days to come, and I prophesied continually of a mighty outpouring.

I had a real ministry to the religious press, and began to attend prayer meetings at the various churches, to exhort them. We were up against it for money, and the devil tempted me to go back to work. Our rent was due, and I had only 50 cents. But the Lord heard prayer. I was about to sell our stove. We had to have a roof over our heads. Just the exact amount we needed came in, without solicitation. God was faithful.

G. Campbell Morgan's little tract on the "Revival in Wales" spread the fire in the churches wonderfully. I did a great deal of visiting among the saints also, and began to sell S. B. Shaw's little book, 'The Great Revival in Wales," among the churches. God wonderfully used it to promote faith for a revival spirit. My tract work was continued among the saloons and business houses.

My clothing by this time was getting quite shabby. In answer to prayer the Lord gave me, through Brother Marsh, a Methodist brother in Pasadena, two second-hand suits of clothes, one light and one heavy, for summer and winter. Both were better than the one I was wearing. So I got a double blessing, twice what I had asked for.

I preached in the M. E. Church at Lamanda Park. Four souls were saved, and others under conviction. One ran out of the meeting to keep from yielding to God. I began to visit more churches, and write more messages for the religious press. The Lord frequently allowed us to be strongly tested financially, but never to make our wants known to the people. We had only a handful of beans in the house on one occasion. But He provided before they were fully consumed. A brother brought us a sack of potatoes as the result of a testimony I gave in the First M. E. Church. It pays to obey God. I preached at Lamanda Park M. E. Church again and the meeting lasted until after midnight. The fire fell. We repaired to the parsonage and were in prayer until near morning.

I owed the landlady for one week's rent. The devil got in her and she ordered me to pay at once, or get out. But God sent the rent. At Lamanda Park I preached a number of times again. The fire fell in a wonderful way. A number of souls were saved. Brother and Sister Frambes, the pastors, were precious children of God. God also began to work at Brother Manley's tent meeting in Pasadena. The burden of prayer was heavy on me for the work in those days. I had little rest day or night, in services and prayer. They were initial days. The fight was on. Both God and the devil were on the move.

May, 1905, I wrote in an article: "My soul is on fire as I read of the glorious work of grace in Wales. The 'seven thousand' in the land, who have kept company with the 'spared ones' (Ezek. 9), and who have been 'crying and sighing' because of the abomination and desolation in the land, the decay of vital piety in the body of Christ, may well be excused for rejoicing at such a time and prospect as this, when God is once more moving in the earth. But where are the men who will 'stir themselves up to take hold on God?' Let our watchword at this time be 'California for Christ.' God is looking for workers, channels, worms of the dust. Remember, He must have worms. Jesus' life was pressed out in prayer at every pore. This kind comes too high for most people. But may not this be our Lord's 'last call?' "

CHAPTER 2

<div align="center">~~~~~~</div>

Pastor Smale
Returns from Wales

June 17, I went to Los Angeles to attend a meeting at the First Baptist Church. They were waiting on God for an outpouring of the Spirit there. Their pastor, Joseph Smale, had just returned from Wales. He had been in touch with the revival and Evan Roberts, and was on fire to have the same visitation and blessing come to his own church in Los Angeles. I found this meeting of an exact piece with my own vision, burden, and desire, and spent two hours in the church in prayer, before the evening service. Meetings were being held every day and night there and God was present.

One afternoon I started the meeting in Los Angeles while they were waiting for Smale to appear. I exhorted them not to wait for man, but to expect from God. They were depending on some great one, the same spirit of idolatry that has cursed the church and hindered God in all ages. Like the children of Israel the people must have "some other god before Him." In State Church circles in Europe the pastor is often known as "the little God." I started the service in the evening on the church steps, outside, while we were waiting for the janitor to arrive with the key. We had a season of prayer for the surrounding community. The evening meeting was a steady sweep of victory.

When God's church becomes what it should be, in love and unity, the doors will never be closed or locked. Like the temple of old it will be always open. (We saw this later, at Azusa Mission.) God has not got 666 churches, all of different names. There is no division in a true "Pentecost," neither in true worship. "God is spirit; and they that worship Him must worship in spirit and truth."—John 4:24. "For by one Spirit are we all baptized into one body; and were all made to drink of one Spirit. —I Cor. 12:13. Ancient Israel, when right with God, were one. How much more should the Church be. We have priests enough to serve continually. And plenty of seeking, needy people to fill the church at all times. How far have we fallen from the early pattern, and even from the type of the church, Israel. We are so short we scarcely recognize the real thing. Even the Roman Church, though formal, is ahead of us in this. The difficulty and shame is that we are hopelessly divided.

I went to Lamanda Park again, and after preaching, spent the night at the parsonage, praying and sleeping alternately. I wanted a fuller revelation of Jesus to my own soul. Like the full moon that draws clearer and nearer to our vision as we continue to steadfastly gaze at it, so Jesus appears more real to our souls as we continue to contemplate Him. We need a closer, personal, vital relationship, acquaintance, and communion with God. Only the man who lives in fellowship with divine reality can be used to call the people to God.

I went to Smale's church again, and again found them listlessly waiting for the preacher to appear. Many did not seem to have any definite idea what they had come to meeting for. I began to pray aloud and the meeting started off with power. It was in full blast when Brother Smale arrived. God wanted the people to look to Him, and not to man. Those not having the glory of God first in view would naturally resent this. But it is God's plan.

We now moved into a little cottage at 175½ N. Vernon Avenue, Pasadena, paying three dollars per month rent, for one room and a small kitchen, unfurnished, without gas or water. I found most Christians did not want to take on a burden of prayer. It was too hard on the flesh. I was carrying this burden now in ever increasing volume, night and day. The ministry was intense. It was "the fellowship of His sufferings," a "travail" of soul, with "groanings that could not be uttered." —Rom. 8:26, 27. Most believers find it easier to criticize than to pray.

One day I was much burdened in prayer. I went to Brother Manley's tent and fell at the altar, there unburdening my soul. A worker ran in from a side tent and begged me to pray for him. I attended another meeting that night and there found a young brother, Edward Boehmer, who had been dug out in the Peniel meetings in the spring, with the same burden of prayer on him. We were wonderfully united in the Spirit from that time on. He was destined to become my prayer helper in the future. We prayed together at the little Peniel Mission until 2 A.M. God wonderfully met and assured us as we wrestled with Him for the outpouring of His Spirit upon the people. My life was by this time literally swallowed up in prayer. I was praying day and night

I wrote more articles for the religious press, exhorting the saints to prayer, and went to Smale's again in Los Angeles. Here I found the people waiting for the preacher again. I was greatly burdened for the situation and tried to show them they must expect from God. Some resented this, being bound by age old custom, but others responded to it. They were praying for a revival like they had in Wales. This was one of the outstanding features there. In Wales they expected from God. The meetings went on whether the preacher was present or absent. They came to meet God. He met them.

I had written a letter to Evan Roberts in Wales, asking them to pray for us in California. I now received a reply that they were doing so, which linked us up with the revival there. The letter read as follows: "My dear brother in the faith: Many thanks for your kind letter. I am impressed of your sincerity and honesty of purpose. Congregate the people together who are willing to make a total surrender. Pray and wait. Believe God's promises. Hold daily meetings. May God bless you, is my earnest prayer. Yours in Christ, Evan Roberts." We were much encouraged to know that they were praying for us in Wales.

I preached at Lamanda Park again, and one night got so blessed while preaching about Elijah's sacrifice that I leaped for joy. I was informed after the service that some of the people were very much shocked at my undignified action, and that they did not want me any more. And they were Methodists at that. God had blessed my ministry much in that place. The devil did not want me to preach any more there. Church fairs and suppers were all right, and in fact all the rage with them at this time. That was "dignified." But I was encouraged when I remembered the fact that neither Wesley nor Fletcher were often allowed to speak the second time in the churches of their day. Many looked upon Fletcher as a monster, when in fact he was one of the most saintly men of his time. Few people really know God in any time.

I went frequently to Brother Smale's church in Los Angeles, taking part in the meetings with much blessing. The Peniel boys went with me and helped to fan the flame. We were much tested at home along financial lines. Money was very tight. But God did not allow us to really suffer. I wrote some articles for the "Way of Faith," the "Christian Harvester," and for "God's Revivalist" at this time. The following are extracts: "A wonderful work of the Spirit has broken out here in Los Angeles, California, preceded by deep preparatory work of prayer and expectation. Conviction is rapidly spreading among the people, and they are rallying from all over the city to the meetings at Pastor Smale's church. Already these meetings are beginning to 'run themselves.' Souls are being saved all over the house, while the meeting sweeps on unguided by human hands. The tide is rising rapidly, and we are anticipating wonderful things. Soul travail is becoming an important feature of the work, and we are being swept away beyond sectarian barriers. The fear of God is coming upon the people, a very spirit of burning. Sunday night the meeting ran on until the small hours of the next morning. Pastor Smale is prophesying of wonderful things to come. He prophesies the speedy return of the apostolic 'gifts' to the church. Los Angeles is a veritable Jerusalem. Just the place for a mighty work of God to begin. I have been expecting just such a display of divine power for some time. Have felt it might break out any hour. Also that it was liable to come where least expected, that God might get the glory. Pray for a 'Pentecost.' —F. Bartleman, June, 1905."

One evening, July 3, I felt strongly impressed to go to the little Peniel Hall in Pasadena to pray. There I found Brother Boehmer ahead of me. He had also been led of God to the hall. We prayed for a spirit of revival for Pasadena until the burden became well nigh unbearable. I cried out like a woman in birth-pangs. The Spirit was interceding through us. Finally the burden left us. After a little time of quiet waiting a great calm settled down upon us. Then suddenly, without premonition, the Lord Jesus himself revealed himself to us. He seemed to stand directly between us, so close we could have reached out our hand and touched him. But we did not dare to move. I could not even look. In fact I seemed all spirit. His presence seemed more real, if possible, than if I could have seen and touched Him naturally. I forgot I had eyes or ears. My spirit recognized Him. A heaven of divine love filled and thrilled my soul. Burning fire went through me. In fact my whole being seemed to flow down bore Him, like wax before the fire. I lost all consciousness of time or space, being conscious only of His wonderful presence. I worshipped at His feet. It seemed a veritable "mount of transfiguration." I was lost in the pure Spirit.

For some time He remained with us. Then slowly He withdrew His presence. We would have been there yet had He not withdrawn. I could not doubt His reality after that experience. Brother Boehmer experienced largely the same thing. We had lost all consciousness of each other's presence while He remained with us. We were almost afraid to speak or breathe when we came back to our surroundings. The Lord had said nothing to us, but only ravished our spirits by His presence. He had come to strengthen and assure us for His service. We knew now we were workers with Him, fellowshippers of his sufferings, in the ministry of "soul travail." Real soul travail is just as definite in the spirit, as natural human birth-pangs. The simile is almost perfect in its sameness. No soul is ever born without this. All true revivals of salvation come this way.

The sun was up next morning before we left the hall. But the night had seemed but half an hour. The presence of God eliminates all sense of time. With Him all is eternity. It is "eternal life." God knows no time. This element is lost in Heaven. This is the secret of time appearing to pass so swiftly in all nights of real prayer. Time is superseded. The element of eternity is there. For days that marvelous presence seemed to walk by my side. The Lord Jesus was so real. I could scarcely take up with human conversation again. It seemed so crude and empty. Human spirits seemed so harsh, earthly fellowship a torment. How far we are naturally from the gentle spirit of Christ!

I spent the following day in prayer, going to Smale's church in the evening, where I had a ministry in intercession. Heavenly peace and joy filled my soul. Jesus was so real. Doubts and fears cannot abide in His presence.

Some one left a load of wood at our door one day, in our absence. We never knew who brought it. We had been praying for wood. I attended Brother Smale's meetings in Los Angeles often and had a blessed ministry in intercession there. God wonderfully poured out his Spirit. Our rent was due again. But a brother wrote out a check for the amount, all unsolicited. We had been praying for it.

I wrote a number of articles to several Holiness papers, describing God's operations among us, and exhorting the saints everywhere to faith and prayer for a revival. The Lord used these articles greatly to bring faith and conviction in many places. I was soon receiving quite a large correspondence, from many places. My concern was chiefly for the Holiness people, that they might not be passed by, and lose the blessing. I wrote in my diary at this time the following observations (a warning to the Pentecostal people): "The Holiness people are loaded down to the water's edge with a spirit of prejudice and pharisaism. But dare we cut ourselves off so easily from other members of the 'body?' We may cut ourselves off from God by our spiritual pride, while He may cause the weakest to repent, and go through to victory. (Referring to the work in the First Baptist Church, at Brother Smale's.) The work in our own hearts must go deeper than we have ever experienced, deep enough to destroy sectarian prejudice, party spirit, etc., on all sides. The work of revival seems to have started outside of the Holiness churches proper. God can perfect those whom He chooses. The Holiness people are too proud of their standing. (Too confident of their position, and condition also.) He may need to pass them by. They must also repent. God may humble them by working in other places."

And history repeats itself. Let the Pentecostal people beware! The present world-wide revival was rocked in the cradle of little Wales. It was 'brought up' in India, following; becoming full grown in Los Angeles later. I received from God early in 1905 the following keynote to revival: **"The depth of revival will be determined exactly by the depth of the spirit of repentance."** And this will obtain for all people, at all times.

The revival spirit at Brother Smale's rapidly spread its interest over the whole city, among the spiritual people. Workers were coming in from all parts, from various affiliations, uniting their prayers with us for a general outpouring. The circle of interest widened rapidly. We were now praying for California, for the Nation, and also for a world-wide revival. The spirit of prophecy began to work among us for mighty things, on a large scale. Some one sent me 5000 pamphlets on "The Revival in Wales." These I distributed among the churches. They had a wonderful quickening influence.

I visited Smale's church again, and started the meeting. He had not yet arrived. The meetings were getting wonderful by this time for their spontaniety. Our little Gideon's band was marching on to certain victory, led by the Captain of their salvation, Jesus. I was led to pray at this early date especially for faith, discernment of spirits, healing, and prophecy. I felt I needed more wisdom and love also. I seemed to receive a real "gift of faith' for the revival at this time, with a spirit of prophecy to the same end, and began to prophesy of mighty things to come.

When we began to pray in the spring of 1905, no one seemed to have much faith for anything out of the ordinary. Pessimism in regard to the then present conditions seemed to obtain generally among the saints. But this condition had changed. God himself had given us faith for better things. There had been nothing in sight to stimulate to this. It came from nothing. And cannot He do the same today?

I wrote an article at this time for the "Daily News" of Pasadena, describing what I saw in Brother Smale's church. It was published and the manager himself came to see soon after. He was greatly convicted, came to the altar, and sought God earnestly. The article was copied in a number of Holiness papers throughout the country. It was entitled, "What I Saw in a Los Angeles Church." The following are some extracts: "For some weeks special services have been held in the First Baptist Church, Los Angeles. Pastor Smale has returned from Wales, where he was in touch with Evan Roberts, and the revival. He registers his conviction that Los Angeles will soon be shaken by the mighty power of God.

"The service of which I am writing began impromptu and spontaneous, some time before the pastor arrived. A handful of people had gathered early, which seemed to be sufficient for the Spirit's operation. The meeting started. Their expectation was from God. God was there, the people were there, and by the time the pastor arrived the meeting was in full swing.

Pastor Smale dropped into his place, but no one seemed to pay any especial attention to him. Their minds were on God. No one seemed to get in another's way, although the congregation represented many religious bodies. All seemed perfect harmony. The Spirit was leading.

"The pastor arose, read a portion of the Scripture, made a few well chosen remarks full of hope and inspiration for the occasion, and the meeting passed again from his hands. The people took it up and went on as before. Testimony, prayer and praise were intermingled throughout the service. The meeting seemed to run itself as far as human guidance was concerned. The pastor was one of them. If one is at all impressionable religiously they must feel in such an atmosphere that something wonderful and imminent is about to take place. Some mysterious, mighty upheaval in the spiritual world is evidently at our doors. The meeting gives one a feeling of "heaven on earth," with an assurance that the supernatural exists, and that in a very real sense."—F. Bartleman, in "Daily News," Pasadena.

I wrote another article, for the "Wesleyan Methodist," at the same time, of which the following are extracts: "Mercy rejected means judgment, and on a corresponding scale. In all the history of God's world there has always been first the offer of divine mercy, then judgment following. First comes Christ on the white horse of mercy. Then follows the red, black and pale horses, of war, famine, and death. The prophets ceased not day and night to faithfully warn Israel, but their tears and entreaties for the most part proved in vain. The awful destruction of Jerusalem, A. D. 70, which resulted in the extermination of a million Jews, and the captivity of multitudes more, was preceded by the offer of divine mercy at the hands of the Son of God himself.

"In 1859, a great revival wave visited our country, sweeping a half million souls into the fountain of salvation. Immediately the terrible carnage of 1861–1865, followed. And so as we anticipate the coming revival, which is already assuming rapidly world-wide proportions, we wonder will not judgment follow mercy, as at other times. And judgment in proportion to the mercy extended. The present warlike attitude and distress of the nations makes us wonder if the judgment to follow may not even plunge us into the 'tribulation,' the Great one." —F. Bartleman, July, 1905.

For "God's Revivalist" I wrote: "Unbelief of every form has come in upon us like a flood. But lo, our God comes also! A standard is being raised against the enemy. The Lord is choosing out His workers. This is a time to realize the vision for service. 'The Lord hath spoken and called the earth from the rising of the sun unto the going down thereof. Our God shall come, and shall not keep silence. Gather my saints together unto me, those who have made a covenant with me by sacrifice.' —Ps. 50." I used often to declare, during 1905, that **I would rather live six months at that time than fifty years of ordinary time.** It was a day of the beginning of great things. For the grain of corn that was willing to "fall into the ground and die," there was promise of abundant harvest. But for spiritual "flappers," the whole matter was naturally foolishness.

I wrote another letter to Evan Roberts, asking for continued prayer for California. Thus we were kept linked up in prayer with Wales for the revival. In those days real prayer was little understood. It was hard to find a quiet place where one would not be disturbed. Gethsemane experiences with Jesus were rare among the saints in those days. And it is fast getting to be the same condition among our Pentecostal missions. In the Azusa

Mission days the first thought for a suitable mission was the prayer room. Now it seems too often to be the last consideration.

At Smale's church one day I was groaning in prayer at the altar. The spirit of intercession was upon me. A brother rebuked me severely. He did not understand it. The flesh naturally shrinks from such ordeals. The "groans" are no more popular in most churches than is a woman in birth-pangs in the home. Soul-travail does not make pleasant company for selfish worldlings. But we cannot have souls born without it. Child bearing is anything but a popular exercise these days. And so with a real revival of new born souls in the churches. Modern society has little place for a child-bearing mother. They prefer society "flappers." And so with the churches regarding soul-travail. There is little burden for souls. Men run from the groans of a woman in travail of birth. And so the church desires no "groans" today. She is too busy enjoying herself.

We were much pressed financially again, but the Lord delivered. We never made our wants known to any one but God, and never begged or borrowed, no matter how pressing the need might seem to be. We believed if the saints were living close enough to God he would speak to them. We trusted Him fully, and went without if He did not send help. I wrote my first tract at this time. It was entitled, "Love Never Faileth." This was the beginning of a large faith tract ministry. I had to trust the Lord for the means. But He never failed me.

I was preaching at various meetings during those days, and had a message on me one day for Brother Manley's meeting. I wanted a quotation of two lines from a volume of Clarke's Commentaries. There were four volumes. Each contained 1000 pages. I only had a few minutes to find it. Prayerfully I chose one of the volumes, closed my eyes and let the book drop open of itself. It was not marked or pressed at that particular page, but wonderful to relate, the book opened exactly at the right place and my eyes fell directly on the quotation that I wanted. This would have been impossible in the natural. I had not at all known where in the book to find it. I only remembered having read it. This strengthened my faith greatly for the message. But I certainly would not, of course, advise this as a practice.

At Brother Smale's church one evening the meeting ran away in the "flesh." He called the people to prayer and the crowd thinned down to one-fourth. Then God came in power. There was too much "religion" there. I ordered a tract printed, "Come Angel Band," and asked the Lord to give me 1000 for a certain price. The printer charged me exactly that amount, knowing nothing of course of my prayer. A sister handed me five dollars. She said the Lord had been talking to her for some time about giving me this. It was the exact amount I had been praying for. I prayed for another five dollars I needed, and a brother soon handed me the exact amount also, without a hint from me on the subject. I trembled to think how wonderfully the Lord was caring for us. My life was wholly at His service. But I dared not be presumptuous.

One evening I went to Brother Manley's tent meeting, without a thought of taking part in the service. I sat in the rear. Soon the Spirit came mightily upon me. I rose and spoke and the power of God fell upon the congregation. The whole company fell on their faces. For three hours the whole tent was an altar service and prayer continued. A number were saved and everybody seemed to get help from God. It was a wonderful visitation of the Spirit. The people were not as rebellious in those days as they are now. They were more willing to have the program broken into, and there were not so many fanatical spirits to hinder. There was a real hunger for God. Almost every night found me taking part in some meeting. The Lord continued to pour out His Spirit.

About this time I had an awful attack of neuralgia of the stomach. I felt I would die. I fasted and prayed a whole day and night and the Lord delivered. It seemed the devil wanted to kill me. I wrote another tract, entitled "That They All May Be One." This stirred the sectarian devil fiercely. But it was Jesus' own prayer—John 17, "that the world may believe."

A friend payed our expenses at the Holiness camp meeting in the Arroyo for a few days, so we tented there. It was mid-summer. We enjoyed the change and outing. I spent most of my time on my face in the woods, in prayer. In the moonlight evenings I poured out my soul unto God, and He met me there. There was much "empty wagon" rattle in the camp. Most were seeking selfish blessings. They rushed to meeting like a big sponge, to get more blessing. They needed stepping on. And so with the Pentecostal people today, largely.

Our cottage rent was due again and the devil fought hard. But God came to our help. Little Ruth was taken very sick at the camp. The weather was hot. We prayed all one night for her and the Lord touched her. I found my soul crying out for God far beyond the seeming aspirations of the most of the Holiness people. I wanted to go deeper, beneath the mere emotional realm, to something more substantial and lasting that would put a rock in my soul. I was tired of so much evanescent froth and foam, so much religious ranting and bombast. And the Lord did not long disappoint me.

The camp meeting committee now got me on the carpet because of the tracts I was distributing in the camp. They thought I was attacking the Holiness movement. But I was only exhorting them to a deeper place in God. They needed more humility and love. My tract against sectarianism, "That They All May Be One," stirred the camp. Surely man-made movements need to be stirred. God has but one "movement," "one body." This was the message at Azusa Mission in the beginning. I received a second letter from Evan Roberts, which read as follows: "Loughor, Wales, 7, 8, 1905. Dear brother: I am very thankful to you for your thoughtful kindness. I was exceedingly pleased to learn the good news of how you are beginning to experience wonderful things. Praying God to continue to bless you, and with many thanks repeated for your good wishes, I am yours in the service. Evan Roberts."

One evening at the Holiness camp the Lord told me he wanted me to preach. I went out in the woods and tried to pray for the meeting. But He said, I want you to preach. I told Him they would not let me. They had a dozen of their own itching for the opportunity. Besides they were half afraid of me. I did not belong to their particular branch of religion. But He said preach! I told Him if He would close every other mouth that night I would obey Him. Throwing the responsibility thus on Him I went to the meeting. It was time for the message. They looked at one another, but every tongue was tied. No one looked at me. The Spirit came upon me and I sprang to my feet. God flooded my soul with power. The message came straight from Him and went like an arrow to the mark. It shook the camp.

Little Ruth was now taken with convulsions and the devil tried to kill her. It was very hot and she was teething. This was the devil's pay for me. We moved back to our cottage in Pasadena again. I mailed eighteen separate packages of my tracts to as many missions on the Pacific Coast. Then God gave me another tract, "The Heart of the Matter." In this I sought to set forth the real object of our worship and faith, Jesus Christ, central preaching, without innuendos. Little Ruth grew worse until we had but small hope in the natural for her life. But God heard our cries and spared her. The enemy seemed determined to rob us of our last remaining child. Financially we were in hard straits also. Not a penny was coming in. But help came, just in the nick of time. God did not fail us. We were trusting Him.

One night the devil came very close to me. I awoke suddenly out of my sleep to find his presence almost as real as my own in the room. I cried to God for help and he fled. Wife felt his presence also, just before I awoke. We were going through a furnace of fire. But the "fourth" was with us. Human help seemed to fail us utterly. The enemy seemed determined to drive me from the work. I was spending whole nights and days in prayer. Evidently Satan's kingdom was suffering. The neighbors hearing me groan in prayer thought I must be sick and inquired of my condition. But it was only soul burden.

The Lord had undertaken wonderfully for me on my last tract. The printer miscalculated and took the job for $6.50 It was worth $9.00. He stood by his bargain. Then he spoiled 1000 by a slight mis-print. These he gave me for almost nothing. I corrected the mistake with my pen.

At Peniel Mission, Los Angeles, a sister spoke to me after the meeting one day, and then passed on. I felt the Lord wanted her to give me some money. I was much in need. So I silently prayed. She stopped about ten feet from me, came back, and handed me one dollar. I was telling a brother of the incident a few minutes later when he told me to wait a minute for him. He went to his room in the mission, and returned at once with two dollars for me. God had heard my prayer.

I went to Smale's church that night, and he resigned. The meetings had run daily in the First Baptist Church for fifteen weeks. It was now September. The officials of the church were tired of the innovation and wanted to return to the old order. He was told to either stop the revival, or get out. He wisely chose the latter. But what an awful position for a church to take, to throw God out. In this same way they later drove the Spirit of God out of the churches in Wales. They tired of His presence, desiring to return to the old, cold, ecclesiastical order. How blind men are! The most spiritual of Pastor Smale's members naturally followed him, with a nucleus of other workers who had gathered to him from other sources, during the revival. They immediately contemplated organizing a New Testament church. I had a feeling perhaps the Lord was cutting Brother Smale loose for the evangelistic field, at least for a time, to spread the fire in other places. But he did not see it so. I had a conference with him with this object in view, and was able to arrange for him to speak at the Lake Avenue M. E. Church, for Pastor Brink, in Pasadena. This had been the storm center of the revival there.

I walked all day spreading the news of the meeting, not having money for carfare, and was so tired at night I could not sleep. We had not a penny, our rent was due, and yet I was literally pouring out my life in the service of God. We had barely the necessities for living. Surely some one must have been failing God. The Lord was wonderfully with me in the Spirit. Many were being blessed by my ministry. The leaders did not encourage me very much. But the humble, hungry souls heard of Jesus gladly. A revival almost always begins among the laity. The ecclesiastical leaders seldom welcome reformation. History repeats itself. The present leaders are too comfortably situated as a rule to desire innovation that might require sacrifice on their part. And God's fire only falls on sacrifice. An empty altar receives no fire. Cold intellectualism, formal ecclesiasticism, and priestly domination are altogether outside the genius of the Gospel. Thank God there are exceptions among the leaders. But we are saved to serve. The true minister is a servant. Jesus came not to be ministered unto, but to minister. Even the mighty evangelist, Chas. G. Finney, was so poor after fifteen years prodigious labors for the Lord that he was obliged to sell his traveling trunk to buy a cow, for the support of his family.

The night before Brother Smale's services at Lake Avenue Church two of us spent the night until after midnight in prayer. Brother Smale preached twice on Sunday. He was wonderfully anointed of God for the occasion. We spent the time between the services in prayer. His message was on the revival in Wales. The people were greatly moved. Brother Smale soon organized a New Testament Church. I became a charter member, as I felt I ought to stay with them, though I did not care very much for the organization.

We got to the point where we had to have money for rent and food, or be turned out to starve. While sitting at my table writing, the Lord spoke and told me to go and see Brother Geo. Crary. The impression was so strong I dropped my pen and went at once. After a season of prayer with Brother Crary and his wife I started to go. I had not said a word about our needs. They handed me $2.50, with the remark that the Lord had sent me there for them to give me this. The devil had tried to run Brother Crary off three times before I got there. But God held him. A little later another brother gave me a dollar. The Lord showed him to do this. So I had three dollars for my rent, and fifty cents to buy food with. We could buy much more for fifty cents in those days than we can now.

One morning soon after this, while we were on our knees praying at home, and in much need of food, the groceryman drove up and left five dollars worth of groceries. He would not tell us who sent it. Some one had paid for it for us. Little Ruth ate a green peach and came near dying again. Prayer saved her. Brother Smale now rented Burbank Hall, and prepared to hold meetings there. I secured the Fourth St. Holiness Hall for him, until Burbank Hall was ready. The Lord gave me another tract, entitled "Pray! Pray! Pray!" I took it to the printer in faith and He sent me the money on time. It was a strong exhortation to prayer. Like the prophets of old we must pray for those who will not pray for themselves. We must confess the sins of the people for them.

At one time while Brother Boehmer and I prayed the Spirit was poured out in a wonderful way in several meetings we were praying for. We felt we had hold of God for them. Following reports proved our convictions. Prayer changes things. There is wonderful power in the proper kind of prayer. Instance Elijah on Mt. Carmel, a man of "like passions" with us. "The effectual fervent prayer of a righteous man availeth much in its working." —Jas. 5:16. Confession may also be necessary in this connection. "Confess therefore your faults one to another."

I now had a cottage offered me in Los Angeles, for eight dollars per month. We had felt for some time the Lord wanted us back in Los Angeles. He sent us the first month's rent, and Brother Penfield in Pasadena loaned me his mule team to move with. We located in the rear of the lot at 619 Towne Avenue. The landlady lived in the front house. It was September 27, 1905.

I was strongly impressed one whole night in prayer to go to San Diego, so I wrote Sister Tillie Haefner, in charge of

Peniel Mission there. The money came in for my fare without solicitation. It was God's will. I preached in Peniel Mission in San Diego, and held street meetings. The police hindered me much, standing in with the saloons, etc. But God gave strength and victory. I visited and prayed with a number of sick people there also, and took a little run over to old Tia Juana, Mexico.

The Burning Bush had spoiled the spirit of the saints greatly in San Diego. It had made them harsh and hard. There was little love, but much strife and contention. God made me a messenger of peace, as usual. I have always stood for the "one body" of Christ. Sister Haefner expressed herself as being much encouraged by my visit. She had had a very hard fight of it. I was taken very sick before I left there, and lay awake all one night with chills and fever. But I had a remarkable experience in this. I had the grippe. Although racked with pain, and burning up with fever, a tremendous spirit of prayer was upon me. I seemed like two separate persons. My brain seemed separate, and alive for God. I felt all spirit. In my body I was sick enough to die. My suffering but seemed to press my soul outside of my body. It was a peculiar experience. I am sure the devil was the loser by it. My spirit seemed completely lifted above my physical condition.

I spoke at the Friends Church Sunday morning on the revival in Wales, and then returned home to Los Angeles. I was so weak I was afraid I would have to be taken from the train on a stretcher. But I got home safely. I had just enough money to get home with. We were up against it financially again. A brother sent me two dollars in a letter, stating the Lord had shown him we were in need. We were praying hard. What a blessed thing to be living where God can speak to one, even though it may cost us something in obedience. Few seem to be living in this place today. Hence the tremendous suffering among God's workers. I am convinced that many true workers are hated bitterly simply because those who feel their prayers, and to whom God is speaking to help them, will not obey the voice of the Lord. Selfishness is a damning sin. Those who give to God cannot possibly lose by it. In fact the only thing we really save is what we give to God. The rest is all lost eventually.

Almost every day in Los Angeles found me engaged in personal work, tract distribution, prayer, or preaching in some meeting. I was writing articles for the religious press continually. I fasted and prayed before going to a tent meeting in Pasadena. The Lord wonderfully anointed me in preaching and twenty souls came to the altar. By this time the spirit of intercession had so possessed me that I prayed almost day and night. I fasted much also, until my wife almost despaired of my life at times. The sorrows of my Lord had gripped me. I was in the Garden with Him. The "travail of His soul" had fallen in a measure on me. I was led to fear, like Him, that I might not live to realize the answer to my prayers and tears for the revival. But He assured me, sending more than one angel to strengthen me, I am satisfied. I felt I was realizing a little of what Paul meant about "filling up the cup of His sufferings" for a lost world. Some were even afraid that I was losing my mind. They could not understand my tremendous concern. Nor can very many understand these things today. "The natural man receiveth not the things of the Spirit." They are "foolishness" unto him. Selfish spirits can never understand such sacrifice. But "he that would save his life shall lose it." "Except a grain of corn fall into the ground and die, etc." Our Lord was a "man of sorrows," as well as of joy.

I frequently went to Pasadena having to trust God for carfare to get home. On one occasion Brother Boehmer had an impression I was coming. He went to the little Peniel Mission and found me there. We spent several hours in prayer. Then he paid my car-fare home. We often spent whole nights together in prayer during those days. It seemed a great privilege to spend a whole night with the Lord. He drew so near. We never seemed to get weary on such occasions. Boehmer worked at gardening. I never asked him for a penny but he always gave me something. God finally not only got his money, but his life also, in His service. He was a wonderful man of prayer. God taught us what it means to "know no man after the flesh." He lifted us into such a high relationship that our fellowship seemed only in the Spirit. Beyond that we died to one another.

I wrote Evan Roberts a third time to have them continue to pray for us in Wales. In those days after I had preached I generally called the saints to their knees and we would be for hours in prayer before we could get up. The Lord led me to write many leaders throughout the country to pray for revival. The spirit of prayer was growing continually. The New Testament Church seemed to be losing the spirit of prayer as they increased their organization. They now tried to shift this ministry on a few of us. I knew God was not pleased with that and became much burdened for them. They had taken on too many secondary interests. It began to look as though the Lord would have to find another body. My hopes had been high for this particular company of people. But the enemy seemed to be sidetracking them now, leading them to miss God's best for them at least.

They were now even attempting to organize prayer, a thing impossible. Prayer is spontaneous. I felt it were better not to have organized than to lose the ministry of prayer and spirit of revival as a body. It was for this they had been called in the beginning. They had become ambitious for a church and organization. It seemed hard to them not to be "like the other nations (churches) 'round about them." And right here they surely began to fail. As church work increased the real issue was lost sight of. And the Pentecostal missions appear to be facing the same danger today. Human organization and human programme leave very little room for the free Spirit of God. It means much to be willing to be considered a failure, while we seek to build up a purely spiritual kingdom. God's kingdom cometh not "by observation."

It is very easy to choose second best. The prayer life is needed much more than even buildings or organizations. These are often a substitute for the other. Souls are born into the kingdom only through prayer.

I feared the New Testament Church might develop a party, sectarian spirit. A rich lady offered them the money to build a church edifice with. The devil was bidding high. But she soon withdrew her offer. I confess I was glad she did. They would soon have had no time for anything but building then. It would have been the end of their revival. We had been called out to evangelize Los Angeles, not to build up another sect or party spirit. We needed no more organization nor machinery than what was really necessary for the speedy evangelizing of the city. Surely we had enough separate rival church organizations already on our hands. Each working largely for its own interest, advancement, and glory.

We had nothing to eat in the house but a little dry bread on one occasion about this time, when I received a letter from Brother Boehmer with a dollar in it. He was in close touch with God. Possibly the saints would do better by the true ones if there were not so many frauds to shake their confidence. Every false shepherd and deceiver in the ranks makes it just that much harder for the true ones.

The New Testament Church seemed to be drifting toward intellectualism. I became much burdened for it. During one meeting I groaned aloud in prayer. It was killing after the meetings we had had. One of the elders rebuked me severely for this. "How are the mighty fallen," kept ringing in my ears. A few of the most spiritual had the same burden with me.

Prayer again seemed to prevail in a measure. We had a great meeting in the church soon after. One hundred knelt at the altar at a single Sunday night service. I met with the Peniel boys in Pasadena for prayer and we had a breaking through time. We felt the Lord would soon work mightily. At Brother Brownley's tent, at Seventh and Spring streets, Los Angeles, we had a deep spirit of prayer and powerful altar services. There was a feeling that God was about to do something extraordinary. The spirit of prayer came more and more heavily upon us. In Pasadena, before moving to Los Angeles, I would lie on my bed in the daytime and roll and groan under the burden. At night I could scarcely sleep for the spirit of prayer. I fasted much, not caring for food while burdened. At one time I was in soul travail for nearly twenty-four hours without intermission. It nearly used me up. Prayer literally consumed me. I would groan all night in my sleep.

Prayer was not formal in those days. It was God breathed. It came upon us, and overwhelmed us. We did not work it up. We were gripped with real soul travail by the Spirit that could no more be shaken off than could the birth-pangs of a woman in travail, without doing absolute violence to the Spirit of God. It was real intercession by the Holy Spirit.

For several days I had an impression another letter was coming from Evan Roberts. It soon came, and read as follows: "Loughor, Wales, Nov. 14, '05. My dear comrade: What can I say that will encourage you in this terrible fight. I find it is a most awful one. The kingdom of the evil one is being besieged on every side. Oh, the millions of prayers—not simply the form of prayer—but the soul finding its way right to the White Throne! People in Wales can pray during the last year. May the Lord bless you with a mighty downpouring. In Wales it seems as if the Holy One rests upon the congregation, awaiting the opening of the hearts of the followers of Christ. We had a mighty downpouring of the Holy Spirit last Saturday night. This was preceded by the correcting of the people's views of true worship. 1.—To give unto God, not to receive. 2.—To please God, not to please ourselves. Therefore looking to God, and forgetting the enemy, and also the fear of men, we prayed, and the Spirit descended. I pray God to hear your prayer, to keep your faith strong, and to save California. I remain, your brother in the fight. Evan Roberts." This was the third letter I had received from Wales, from Evan Roberts, and I feel their prayers had much to do with our final victory in California.

Evan Roberts tells us of his own experience with God: "One Friday night last spring, while praying by my bedside before retiring, I was taken up to a great expanse, without time or space. It was communion with God. Before this I had had a far off God. I was frightened that night, but never since. So great was my shivering that I rocked the bed, and my brother, being awakened, took hold of me, thinking I was ill." This experience took place every night after this with Evan Roberts, for three months, from 1 o'clock until 5. He wrote a message to the world about this time, as follows: The revival in South Wales is not of men, but of God. He has come very close to us. There is no question of creed or of dogma in this movement. We are teaching no sectarian doctrine, only the wonder and beauty of Christ's love. I have been asked concerning my methods. I have none. I never prepare what I shall speak, but leave that to Him. I am not the source of this revival, but only one agent among what is growing to be a multitude. I wish no personal following, but only the world for Christ. I believe that the world is upon the threshold of a great religious revival, and pray daily that I may be allowed to help bring this about. Wonderful things have happened in Wales in a few weeks, but these are only a beginning. The world will be swept by His Spirit as by a rushing, mighty wind. Many who are now silent Christians will lead the movement. They will see a great light, and will reflect this light to thousands now in darkness. Thousands will do more than we have accomplished, as God gives them power." —Evan Roberts. What beautiful humility! This is the secret of all power.

An English eye-witness writes of the revival in Wales: "Such real travail of soul for the unsaved I have never before witnessed. I have seen young Evan Roberts convulsed with grief, and calling on his audience to pray. 'Don't sing,' he would exclaim, 'it's too terrible to sing.'" (Conviction has often been lifted from the people by too much singing.)

Another writer declares it was not the eloquence of Evan Roberts that broke men down, but his tears. He would break down, crying bitterly for God to bend them, in an agony of prayer, the tears coursing down his cheeks, with his whole frame writhing. Strong men would break down and cry like children. Women would shriek. A sound of weeping and wailing would fill the air. Evan Roberts in the intensity of his agony would fall in the pulpit, while many in the crowd often fainted."

Of the later work in India we read: "The girls in India so wonderfully wrought upon and baptized with the Spirit (in

Ramabai's mission), began by terrifically beating themselves, under pungent conviction of their need. Great light was given them. When delivered they jumped up and down for joy, for hours without fatigue, in fact were stronger for it. They cried out with the burning that came into and upon them. Some fell as they saw a great light pass before them, while the fire of God burned the members of the body of sin, pride, anger, love of the world, selfishness, uncleanness, etc. They neither ate nor slept until the victory was won. Then the joy was so great that for two or three days after receiving the baptism of the Holy Spirit they did not care for food. About twenty girls went into a trance at one time and became unconscious of this world for hours; some for three or four days. During that time they sang, prayed, clapped their hands, rolled about, or sat still. When they became conscious they told of seeing a throne in Heaven, a white robed throng, and a glory so bright they could not bear it. Soon the whole place was aflame. School had to be suspended, they forgot to eat or sleep, and whole nights and days were absorbed in prayer. The Spirit was poured out upon one of the seeking girls in the night. Her companion sleeping next to her awoke, and seeing fire envelop her, ran across the dormitory and brought a pail of water to dash upon her. In less than an hour nearly all the girls in the compound were weeping, praying, and confessing their sins. Many of these girls were invested with a strange, beautiful and supernatural fire."

The spontaneous composition of hymns was a curious feature of some of the meetings in other parts of India. At Kara Camp pictures appeared on the walls to a company of small girls in prayer, supernaturally depicting the life of Christ. The figures moved in the pictures and were in colors. Each view would last from two to ten minutes and then the light would gradually fade away, to reappear in a few moments with a new scene. These appeared for twelve hours, and were not only seen by the native children of the orphanage and eight missionaries, but by native Christians living near, and even heathen coming to see the wonderful sight. These pictures were all depicting faithfully the Bible narration and were entirely supernatural. They had a tremendous effect in breaking up the hard hearts of the heathen. In Wales colored lights were often seen, like balls of fire, during the revival there.

I kept going day and night to different missions, exhorting continually to prayer, and faith for the revival. Spent another whole night with Brother Boehmer in prayer. One night at the New Testament Church, during a deep spirit of prayer on the congregation, the Lord came suddenly so near that we could feel His presence as though he were closing in on us around the edges of the meeting. Two-thirds of the people sprang to their feet in alarm, and some ran hurriedly out of the house, even leaving their hats behind them, almost scared out of their senses. There was no demonstration in the natural out of the ordinary to cause this fright. It was a supernatural manifestation of His nearness. What would such do if they saw the Lord

I started a little cottage prayer meeting where we could have more liberty to pray and wait on the Lord. The spirit of prayer was being hindered in the meetings. The more spiritual were hungry for this opportunity. But the leaders misunderstood me and opposed me. Then our landlady got the devil in her and wanted to throw us out of our home. She was not right with God. Our rent was paid up. But the enemy tried to use her. The fight was on. They began to oppose my ministry at the New Testament Church. A sister tried to persuade me to discontinue the prayer meetings I had started. I asked the Lord to show me

His will in the matter. He came and filled our little cottage with a cloud of glory until I could scarcely bear His presence. That settled it for me. "We ought to obey God rather than men." I suffered much criticism at this time. I think they were afraid I would start another church. But I had no such thought at that time. I only wanted to have freedom to pray. Many a mission and church has gone on the rocks opposing God.

I wrote more articles for the religious press, of which the following are extracts: "Slowly but surely the conviction is coming upon the saints of Southern California that God is going to pour out His Spirit here as in Wales. We are having faith for things such as we have never dreamed of, for the near future. We are assured of no less than a "Pentecost" for this whole country. But we can never have pentecostal results without pentecostal power. And this will mean pentecostal demonstration. Few care to meet God face to face. "Flesh and blood cannot inherit the kingdom of God."—Christian Harvester.

Again I wrote: "The current of revival is sweeping by our door. Will we cast ourselves on its mighty bosom and ride to glorious victory? **A year of life at this time, with its wonderful possibilities for God, is worth a hundred years of ordinary life.** 'Pentecost' is knocking at our doors. The revival for our country is no longer a question. Slowly but surely the tide has been rising until in the very near future we believe for a deluge of salvation that will sweep all before it. Wales will not long stand alone in this glorious triumph for our Christ. The spirit of reviving is coming upon us, driven by the breath of God, the Holy Ghost. The clouds are gathering rapidly, big with a mighty rain, whose precipitation lingers but a little.

"Heroes will arise from the dust of obscure and despised circumstances, whose names will be emblazoned on Heaven's eternal page of fame. The Spirit is brooding over our land again as at creation's dawn, and the fiat of God goes forth. 'Let there be light.' Brother, sister, if we all believed God can you realize what would happen? Many of us here are living for nothing else. A volume of believing prayer is ascending to the throne night and day. Los Angeles, Southern California, and the whole continent shall surely find itself ere long in the throes of a mighty revival, by the Spirit and power of God." —F. Bartleman, in "Way of Faith," Nov. 16, 1905.

December 14, I was 34 years old. I felt I had done so little in my time for God. I longed to be used for Him more definitely. There was not a penny in the house, and we had no milk for little Ruth. But God got help through to us, after a fierce battle in prayer. The answer is often hindered today, even as in Daniel's time. The devil influences the saints to hold back. I went to a tent meeting and preached and the fire fell in the camp. Souls were saved. We had been for some time led to pray for a Pentecost. It seemed almost beginning. Of course we did not realize what a real "Pentecost" was. But the Spirit did, and led us to ask aright.

I had been praying for a fountain pen. A brother found one and gave it to me. He already had one. I wrote thirty letters of exhortation to prayer and faith for a revival, to as many missions, on the coast and in foreign fields. But I had no postage. While I was writing a sister came in and handed me four dollars. I had asked for a witness if the letters were from Him. I was given several more articles for the religious press. After spending another whole night in prayer with Brother Boehmer I was given a message of exhortation which I delivered in a number of churches and missions.

I felt the New Testament Church was failing God, and was looking to see where the Spirit might come forth. They

it myself. We had been praying for just this thing, but he had not known it. So we moved April 13 to 714 East Thirty-first street. It seemed like a palace after living in two-room shacks and sheds. God was wonderfully providing for us.

The latter part of March the Lord had given me another tract, entitled "The Last Call." This was used mightily to awaken the people. The following are some extracts: "And now, once more, at the very end of the age, God calls. The Last Call, the Midnight Cry, is now upon us, sounding clearly in our ears. God will give this one more chance, the last. A final call, a world-wide Revival. Then Judgment upon the whole world. Some tremendous event is about to transpire, etc."

CHAPTER 3

The Fire Falls at "Azusa"

I went to Burbank Hall, the New Testament Church, Sunday morning, April 15. A colored sister was there and spoke in "tongues." This created a great stir. The people gathered in little companies on the sidewalk after the service inquiring what this might mean. It seemed like Pentecostal "signs." We then learned that the Spirit had fallen a few nights before, April 9, at the little cottage on Bonnie Brae street. They had been tarrying very earnestly for some time for an outpouring. A handful of colored and white saints had been waiting there daily. It was just at Easter season again. For some reason I was not privileged to be present at that particular meeting. A number had spoken in "tongues" there. I went to the Bonnie Brae meeting in the afternoon, and found God working mightily. We had been praying for many months for victory. Jesus was now "showing himself alive" again, to many. The pioneers had broken through, for the multitude to follow.

There was a general spirit of humility manifested in the meeting. They were taken up with God. Evidently the Lord had found the little company at last, outside as always, through whom he could have right of way. There was not a mission in the country where this could be done. All were in the hands of men. The Spirit could not work. Others far more pretentious had failed. That which man esteems had been passed by once more and the Spirit born again in a humble "stable," outside ecclesiastical establishments as usual.

A body must be prepared, in repentance and humility, for every outpouring of the Spirit. The preaching of the Reformation was begun by Martin Luther in a tumble down building in the midst of the public square in Wittemberg. D'Aubigne describes it as follows: "In the middle of the square at Wittemberg stood an ancient wooden chapel, thirty feet long and twenty wide, whose walls, propped up on all sides, were falling into ruin. An old pulpit made of planks, and three feet high, received the preacher. It was in this wretched place that the preaching of the Reformation began. It was God's will that that which was to restore His glory should have the humblest surroundings. It was in this wretched enclosure that God willed, so to speak, that his well-beloved Son should be born a second time. Among those thousands of cathedrals and parish churches with which the world is filled, there was not one at that time which God chose for the glorious preaching of eternal life."

In the revival in Wales the great expounders of England had to come and sit at the feet of crude, hard working miners, and see the wonderful works of God. I wrote for the "Way of Faith" at this time: "The real thing is appearing among us. The Almighty will again measure swords with Pharaoh's magicians. But many will reject Him and blaspheme. Many will fail to recognize Him, even among His professed followers. We have been praying and believing for a 'Pentecost.' Will we receive it when it comes?

The present Pentecostal manifestation did not break out in a moment, like a huge prairie fire, and set the world on fire.

In fact no work of God ever appears that way. There is a necessary time for preparation. The finished article is not realized at the beginning. Men may wonder where it came from, not being conscious of the preparation, but there is always such. Every movement of the Spirit of God must also run the gauntlet of the devil's forces. The Dragon stands before the bearing mother, ready to swallow up her child. —(Rev. 12:4.) And so with the present Pentecostal work in its beginning. The enemy did much counterfeiting. God kept the young child well hid for a season from the Herods, until it could gain strength and discernment to resist them. The flame was guarded jealously by the hand of the Lord, from the winds of criticism, jealousy, unbelief, etc. It went through about the same experiences that all revivals have. Its foes were both inside and out. Both Luther and Wesley experienced the same difficulties in their time. We have this treasure in "earthen vessels." Every natural birth is surrounded by circumstances not entirely pleasant. God's perfect work is wrought in human imperfection. We are creatures of "the fall." Then why expect a perfect manifestation in this case? We are coming " back to God."

John Wesley writes of his time: "Almost as soon as I was gone two or three began to take their imaginations for impressions from God. Meantime, a flood of reproach came upon me almost from every quarter. Be not alarmed that Satan sows tares among the wheat of Christ. It has ever been so, especially on any remarkable outpouring of the Spirit; and ever will be, until the devil is chained for a thousand years. Till then he will always ape, and endeavor to counteract the work of the Spirit of Christ." D'Aubigne has said: "A religious movement almost always exceeds a just moderation. In order that human nature may make one step in advance, its pioneers must take many."

Another writer says: "Remember with what accompaniments of extravagance and fanaticism the doctrine of justification by faith was brought back under Luther. The wonder was, not that Luther had the courage to face pope and cardinals, but that he had courage to endure the contempt which his own doctrines brought upon him, as espoused and paraded by fanatical advocates. Recall the scandal and offense which attended the revival of heart piety under Wesley. What we denounce as error may be "the refraction of some great truth below the horizon."

John Wesley himself once prayed, after the revival had about died out for the time: "Oh, Lord, send us the old revival, without the defects; but if this cannot be, send it—with all its defects. We must have the revival."

Adam Clark said: "Nature will always, and Satan too, mingle themselves as far as they can, in the genuine work of the Spirit, in order to discredit and destroy it. Nevertheless in great revivals of religion, it is almost impossible to prevent wild-fire from getting in among the true fire."

Dr. Seiss says: "Never, indeed, has there been a sowing of God on earth, but it has been oversown by Satan; or a growth for Christ, which the plantings of the wicked one did not mingle with and hinder. He who sets out to find a perfect church, in which there are no unworthy elements, and no disfigurations, proposes to himself a hopeless task."

Still another writer says: "In the various crises that have occured in the history of the church, men have come to the front who have manifested a holy recklessness that astonished their fellows. When Luther nailed his theses to the door of the cathedral at Wittemberg, cautious men were astonished at his audacity. When John Wesley ignored all church restrictions and religious propriety and preached in the fields and by-ways, men declared his reputation was ruined. So it has been in all ages. When the religious condition of the times called for men who were willing to sacrifice all for Christ, the demand created the supply, and there have always been found a few who were willing to be regarded reckless for the Lord. An utter reckless-ness concerning men's opinions and other consequences is the only attitude that can meet the exigencies of the present times." God found His Moses, in the person of Brother Smale, to lead us to the Jordan crossing. But He chose Brother Seymour, for our Joshua, to lead us over.

Sunday, April 15, the Lord called me to ten days of special prayer. I felt greatly burdened but had no idea of what He had particularly in mind. But He had a work for me, and wanted to prepare me for it. Wednesday, April 18, the terrible San Francisco earthquake came, which also devastated the surrounding cities and country. No less than ten thousand lost their lives in San Francisco alone. I felt a deep conviction that the Lord was answering our prayers for a revival in His own way. "When Thy judgments are in the earth, the inhabitants of the world learn righteousness." —Isa. 26:9. A tremendous burden of prayer came upon me that the people might not be indifferent to His voice.

Thursday, April 19, while sitting in the noon meeting at Peniel Hall, 227 South Main street, the floor suddenly began to move with us. A most ugly sensation ran through the room. We sat in awe. Many people ran into the middle of the street, looking up anxiously at the buildings, fearing they were about to fall. It was an earnest time. I went home and after a season of prayer was impressed of the Lord to go to the meeting which had been removed from Bonnie Brae street to 312 Azusa street.

Here they had rented an old frame building, formerly a Methodist church, in the center of the city, now a long time out of use for meetings. It had become a receptacle for old lumber, plaster, etc. They had cleared space enough in the surrounding dirt and debris to lay some planks on top of empty nail kegs, with seats enough for possibly thirty people, if I remember rightly. These were arranged in a square, facing one another.

I was under tremendous pressure to get to the meeting that evening. It was my first visit to "Azusa Mission." Mother Wheaton, who was living with us, was going with me. She was so slow that I could hardly wait for her. I have always been a "lone wolf" for this very reason. My time is not my own. I am His servant. "The King's business requires haste." We cannot wait all day for some one to get ready who neither has the orders, nor feels the necessity. "Salute no man by the way." God's business is important. He requires obedience. Thus we also keep out of some one else's way. There is too much involved to fail God. Let those take their time and come behind who have no message. The devil can often use them tremendously to hinder those who have.

We finally reached "Azusa" and found about a dozen saints there, some white, some colored. Brother Seymour was there, in charge. The "Ark of God" moved off slowly, but surely, at "Azusa." It was carried "on the shoulders" of His own appointed priests in the beginning. We had no "new cart" in those days, to please the carnal, mixed multitude. We had the devil to fight, but the Ark was not drawn by oxen (dumb beasts). The priests were "alive unto God," through much preparation and prayer. Discernment was not perfect, and the enemy got some advantage, which brought reproach to the work, but the saints soon learned to "take the precious from the vile." The combined forces of hell were set determinedly against us in the beginning. It was not all blessing. In fact the fight was terrific. The devil scraped the country for crooked spirits, as always, to destroy the work if possible. But the fire could not be smothered. Strong saints were gathered together to the help of the Lord. Gradually the tide arose in victory. But from a small beginning, a very little flame.

I gave a message at my first meeting at "Azusa." Two of the saints spoke in "tongues." Much blessing seemed to attend the utterance. It was soon noised abroad that God was working at "Azusa." All classes began to flock to the meetings. Many were curious and unbelieving, but others were hungry for God. The newspapers began to ridicule and abuse the meetings, thus giving us much free advertising. This brought the crowds. The devil overdid himself again. Outside persecution never hurt the work. We had the most to fear from the working of evil spirits within. Even spiritualists and hypnotists came to investigate, and to try their influence. Then all the religious sore-heads and crooks and cranks came, seeking a place in the work. We had the most to fear from these. But this is always the danger to every new work. They have no place elsewhere. This condition cast a fear over many which was hard to overcome. It hindered the Spirit much. **Many were afraid to seek God, for fear the devil might get them.**

We found early in the "Azusa" work that when we attempted to steady the Ark the Lord stopped working. We dared not call the attention of the people too much to the working of the evil. Fear would follow. We could only pray. Then God gave victory. There was a presence of God with us, through prayer, we could depend on. The leaders had a limited experience, and the wonder is the work survived at all against its powerful adversaries. But it was of God. That was the secret.

A certain writer has well said: "On the day of Pentecost, Christianity faced the world, a new religion—without a college, a people, or a patron. All that was ancient and venerable rose up before her in solid opposion. And she did not flatter or conciliate any one of them. She assailed every existing system, and every bad habit, burning her way through innumerable forms of opposition. This she accomplished with her "tongue of fire" alone.

Another writer has said: "The apostacy of the early church came as a result of a greater desire to see the spread of its power and rule than to see new natures given to its individual members. The moment we covet a large following and rejoice in the crowd that is attracted by our presentation of what we consider truth, and have not a greater desire to see the natures of individuals changed according to the divine plan, we start to travel the same road of apostacy that leads to Rome and her daughters."

I found the earthquake had opened many hearts. I was distributing especially my last tract, "The Last Call." It seemed very appropriate after the earthquake. Sunday, April 22, I took 10,000 of these to the New Testament Church. The workers seized them eagerly and scattered them quickly throughout the city.

Nearly every pulpit in the land was working overtime to prove that God had nothing to do with earthquakes and thus allay the fears of the people. The Spirit was striving to knock at hearts with conviction, through this judgment. I felt indignation that the preachers should be used of Satan to drown out His voice. Just as he later used them to stir up hatred and murder, during the great war. Even the teachers in the schools labored hard to convince the children that God was not in earthquakes. The devil put on a big propaganda on this line.

I had been much in prayer since the earthquake, and had slept little. After the shock in Los Angeles the Lord told me definitely he had a message for me for the people. On the Saturday after, He gave me a part of it. On Monday the rest was given. I finished writing it at 12:30 A. M. Tuesday, ready for the printer. I kneeled before the Lord and He met me in a powerful way, a powerful witness that the message was from Him. I was to have it printed in the morning. From that time until 4 A. M., I was wonderfully taken up in the spirit of intercession. I seemed to feel the wrath of God against the people and to withstand it in prayer. He showed me he was terribly grieved at their obstinacy in the face of his judgment on sin. San Francisco was a terribly wicked city.

He showed me all hell was being moved to drown out His voice in the earthquake, if possible. The message He had given me was to counteract this influence. Men had been denying His presence in the earthquake. Now He would speak. It was a terrific message He had given me. I was to argue the question with no man , but simply give them the message. They would answer to Him. I felt all hell against me in this, and so it proved. I went to bed at 4 o'clock, arose at 7, and hurried with the message to the printer.

The question in almost every heart was, "Did God do that?" But instinct taught men on the spot that He had. Even the wicked were conscious of the fact. The tract was set up quickly. The same day it was on the press, and the next noon I had my first consignment of the tract. I was impressed I must hasten and get them to the people as quickly as possible. I was reminded that the ten days I was called by the Lord to prayer was up the very day I received the first of the tracts. I understood it all now, clearly.

The enemy tried to hinder, by smashing a part of the type in the press. I had warned the printer of this. But it was set up again so that I lost no time through it. I distributed the message speedily in the missions, churches, saloons, business houses, and in fact everywhere, both in Los Angeles and Pasadena. Besides I mailed thousands to workers in nearby towns for distribution. The whole undertaking was a work of faith. I began without a dollar. But He supplied the money, as needed. I worked hard every day. Brother and Sister Otterman distributed them in San Diego. It required courage. Many raved at the message. I went through all the dives with them in Los Angeles. All hell was stirred. A man followed me on the street raving like a maniac. He followed me into a business house, to do me violence. But the Lord protected. He then tore my tract up publicly at the curb, to show his hate. Many threw the message down in a rage, only to pick it up again and read it. It seemed God held them to it. The saddest part was the fact that nearly all the preachers worked with the enemy in the matter. But I was only giving them the Word of God, on earthquakes.

I ordered the tracts in 25,000 lots. A policeman was put on my track. The people were stirred up so. But the Spirit warned me and I saw him coming. I was enabled to dodge him. He would have stopped the circulation of the tract before my work was done. I could feel hell's rage rolling up against me like a cloud. But God gave me courage for the work. Hundreds were distributed in Santa Barbara. A conductor stopped me giving them out on a Pasadena car, though the people were reaching out their hands for them. He threatened to throw me off the car.

The devil was stirred. Order came in for thousands from towns in Southern California, which I mailed to them. Everyone was curious for the tract, though it burned the most of them like fire. Sometimes they would get so excited on the street cars they would get off before they reached their street. My very presence seemed to convict many. My soul was steeped in prayer. The message struck consternation to thousands of souls. I have never written a tract that had so much influence.

God sent Brother Boehmer from Pasadena to help me. He stood outside and prayed while I went into the saloons with them. They were mad enough to kill me in some instances. Business was at a standstill after the news came from San Francisco. The people were paralyzed with fear. This accounted to some extent for the influence of my tract. The pressure against me was terrific. All hell was surging around me, to stop the message. But I never faltered. I felt God's hand upon me continually in the matter. The people were appaled to see what God had to say about earthquakes. He sent me to a number of meetings with a solemn exhortation to repent and seek Him. At "Azusa Mission" we had a powerful time. The saints humbled themselves. A colored sister both spoke and sang in "tongues." The very atmosphere of Heaven was there.

Sunday, May 11, I had finished my "Earthquake" tract distribution. Then the burden suddenly left me. My work was done. Seventy-five thousand had been published and distributed in Los Angeles and Southern California, in less than three weeks' time. At Oakland, Brother Manley, of his own volition, had printed and distributed 50,000 more, in the Bay Cities and 'round about, in about the same space of time. The following are some extracts from the "Earthquake" tract: "But what has God to do with earthquakes? 'When Thy judgments

are in the earth, the inhabitants of the world learn righteousness.' —Isa. 26:9. 'Which removeth the mountains, when He
overturneth them in His anger, which shaketh the earth out of
her place, and the pillars thereof tremble.' —Job 9:5, 6. 'The
mountains quake at Him, and the hills melt; and the earth is
upheaved at His presence, yea, the world, and all that dwell
therein. His fury is poured out like fire, and the rocks are broken
asunder by Him.' —Nahum 1:5, 6. 'And I will punish the world
for their evil. Therefore I will make the heavens to tremble,
and the earth shall be shaken out of her place, in the day of His
fierce anger.' —Isa. 13:11, 13. 'Then the earth shook and trembled, the foundations also of the mountains moved, and were
shaken, because He was wroth. There went up a smoke in His
wrath, and fire out of His mouth devoured. The Lord thundered
from Heaven, and the Most High uttered His voice. Then the
channels of the sea appeared, the foundations of the world were
laid bare, by the rebuke of the Lord, at the blast of the breath of
His anger.' —Ps. 18. 'Behold, the Lord maketh the earth empty,
and turneth it upside down (perverteth the face thereof), and
scattereth abroad the inhabitants thereof. The foundations
of the earth do shake, the earth is utterly broken, the earth
is moved exceedingly. The earth shall stagger like a drunken
man, and shall be moved to and fro. The transgression thereof
shall be heavy upon it.' —Isa. 24:1, 18, 20. 'Thou shalt be visited of the Lord of Hosts with earthquakes, and great noise,
and the flame of a devouring fire.' —Isa. 29:6. 'Men shall go
into the caves of the rocks, from before the terror of the Lord,
when he arises to shake terribly the earth.' —Isa. 2:19. 'And
the seventh angel poured out his vial into the air and there
was a great earthquake.' —Rev. 16:17, 18. And will you claim
there is no God in earthquakes? John Wesley has said, 'Of all

the judgments which the righteous God inflicts on sinners here, the most dreadful and destructive is an earthquake.'" —From "Earthquake Tract," April, 1906.

The San Francisco earthquake was surely the voice of God to the people on the Pacific Coast. It was used mightily in conviction, for the gracious after revival. In the early "Azusa" days both Heaven and hell seemed to have come to town. Men were at the breaking point. Conviction was mightily on the people. They would fly to pieces even on the street, almost without provocation. A very "dead line" seemed to be drawn around "Azusa Mission," by the Spirit. When men came within two or three blocks of the place they were seized with conviction. I took a run to San Diego and preached twice a day for Brother and Sister Otterman. The Lord blessed my ministry, and the change was a blessing, after the tremendous strain I had been under. I had asked the Lord for my fare if He wanted me to go, and He gave it. It was now June. Returning home I distributed tracts at the Free Methodist camp meeting. I asked the Lord for ten dollars, and he gave me twenty.

The work was getting clearer and stronger at "Azusa." God was working mightily. It seemed that every one had to go to "Azusa." Missionaries were gathered there from Africa, India, and the islands of the sea. Preachers and workers had crossed the continent, and come from distant islands, with an irresistible drawing to Los Angeles. "Gather my saints together, etc." —Ps. 50:1–7. They had come up for "Pentecost," though they little realized it. It was God's call. Holiness meetings, tents and missions began to close up for lack of attendance. Their people were at "Azusa." Brother and Sister Garr closed the "Burning Bush" hall, came to "Azusa," received the "baptism," and were soon on their way to India to spread the fire. Even Brother Smale had to come to "Azusa," to look up his members. He invited them back home, promised them liberty in the Spirit, and for a time God wrought mightily at the New Testament Church also.

There was much persecution, especially from the press. They wrote us up shamefully, but this only drew the crowds. Some gave the work six months to live. Soon the meetings were running day and night. The place was packed out nightly. The whole building, upstairs and down, had now been cleared and put into use. There were far more white people than colored coming. The "color line" was washed away in the blood. A. S. Worrell, translator of the New Testament, declared the "Azusa" work had rediscovered the blood of Christ to the church at that time. Great emphasis was placed on the "blood," for cleansing, etc. A high standard was held up for a clean life. "When the enemy shall come in like a flood, the Spirit of the Lord shall lift up a standard against him." —Isa. 59:19. Divine love was wonderfully manifest in the meetings. They would not even allow an unkind word said against their opposers, or the churches. The message was the love of God. It was a sort of "first love" of the early church returned. The "baptism" as we received it in the beginning did not allow us to think, speak, or hear evil of any man. The Spirit was very sensitive, tender as a dove. The Holy Spirit is symbolized as a dove. A dove has no gall bladder. We knew the moment we had grieved the Spirit, by an unkind thought or word. We seemed to live in a sea of pure divine love. The Lord fought our battles for us in those days. We committed ourselves to His judgment fully in all matters, never seeking to even defend the work or ourselves. We lived in His wonderful, immediate presence. And nothing contrary to His pure Spirit was allowed there.

The false was sifted out from the real by the Spirit of God. The Word of God itself decided absolutely all issues. The hearts of the people, both in act and motive, were searched to the very bottom. It was no joke to become one of that company. No man "durst join himself to them" except he meant business, to go through. It meant a dying out and cleaning up process in those days, to receive the "baptism." We had a "tarrying" room upstairs, for those especially seeking God for the "baptism," though many got it in the main assembly room also. In fact they often got it in their seats in those days. On the wall of the tarrying room was hung a placard with the words, "No talking above a whisper." We knew nothing of "jazzing" them through at that time. The Spirit wrought very deeply. An unquiet spirit, or a thoughtless talker, was immediately reproved by the Spirit. We were on "holy ground." This atmosphere was unbearable to the carnal spirit. They generally gave this room a wide berth unless they had been thoroughly sudued and burned out. Only honest seekers sought it, those who really meant business with God. It was no "lethal chamber," nor place to throw fits, or blow off steam in. Men did not "fly to their lungs" in those days. They flew to the mercy seat. They took their shoes off, figuratively speaking. They were on "holy ground." "Fools rush in where angels fear to tread."

Arthur Booth-Clibborn has written the following weighty words for the "Pentecostal" people: "Any cheapening of the price of Pentecost would be a disaster of untold magnitude. The company in the upper room, upon whom Pentecost fell, had paid for it the highest price. In this they approached as near as possible to Him who had paid the supreme price in order to send it. Do we ever really adequately realize how utterly lost to this world, how completely despised, rejected and outcast was that company? Their master and leader had just passed, so to speak, through the 'hangman's rope,' at the hands of the highest civilization of the day. Their Calvary was complete, and so a complete Pentecost came to match it. The latter will resemble the former in completeness. We may, therefore, each of us say to ourselves: As thy cross, so will thy Pentecost be. God's way to Pentecost was via Calvary. Individually it must be so today also. The purity and fulness of the individual Pentecost must depend upon the completeness of the individual Calvary. This is an unalterable principle."

Friday, June 15, at "Azusa," the Spirit dropped the "heavenly chorus" into my soul. I found myself suddenly joining the rest who had received this supernatural "gift." It was a spontaneous manifestation and rapture no earthly tongue can describe. In the beginning this manifestation was wonderfully pure and powerful. We feared to try to reproduce it, as with the "tongues" also. Now many seemingly have no hesitation in imitating all the "gifts." They have largely lost their power and influence because of this. No one could understand this "gift of song" but those who had it. It was indeed a "new song," in the Spirit. When I first heard it in the meetings a great hunger entered my soul to receive it. I felt it would exactly express my pent up feelings. I had not yet spoken in "tongues." But the "new song" captured me. It was a gift from God of high order, and appeared among us soon after the "Azusa" work began. No one had preached it. The Lord had sovereignly bestowed it, with the outpouring of the "residue of oil," the "Latter Rain" baptism of the Spirit. It was exercised, as the Spirit moved the possessors, either in solo fashion, or by the company. It was sometimes without words, other times in "tongues." The effect was wonderful on the people. It brought a heavenly atmosphere, as though the angels themselves were present and joining with us. And possibly they were. It seemed to still criticism and opposition, and was hard for even wicked men to gainsay or ridicule.

Some have condemned this "new song," without words. But was not sound given before language? And is there not intelligence without language also? Who composed the first song? Must we necessarily follow some man's composition, before us, always? We are too much worshippers of tradition. The speaking in "tongues" is not according to man's wisdom or understanding. Then why not a "gift of song?" It is certainly a rebuke to the "jazzy" religious songs of our day. And possibly it was given for that purpose. Yet some of the old hymns are very good to sing, also. We need not despise or treat lightly of them. Some one has said that every fresh revival brings in its own hymnology. And this one surely did.

In the beginning in "Azusa" we had no musical instruments. In fact we felt no need of them. There was no place for them in our worship. All was spontaneous. We did not even sing from hymn books. All the old, well known hymns were sung from memory, quickened by the Spirit of God. "The Comforter Has Come," was possibly the one most sung. We sang it from fresh, powerful heart experience. Oh, how the power of God filled and thrilled us. Then the "blood" songs were very popular. "The life is in the blood." Sinai, Calvary, and Pentecost, all had their rightful place in the "Azusa" work. But the "new song" was altogether different, not of human composition. It cannot be successfully counterfeited. The crow cannot imitate the dove. But they finally began to despise this "gift," when the human spirit asserted itself again. They drove it out by hymn books, and selected songs by leaders. It was like murdering the Spirit, and most painful to some of us, but the tide was too strong against us. Hymn books today are largely a commercial proposition, and we would not lose much without most of them. The old tunes, even, are violated by change, and new styles must be gotten out every season, for added profit. There is very little real spirit of worship in them. They move the toes, but not the hearts of men. The spirit of song given from God in the beginning was like the Aeolian harp, in its spontaniety and sweetness. In fact it was the very breath of God, playing on human heart strings, or human vocal cords. The notes were wonderful in sweetness, volume and duration. In fact they were oftimes humanly impossible. It was "singing in the Spirit."

Brother Seymour was recognized as the nominal leader in charge. But we had no pope or hierarchy. We were "brethren." We had no human programme. The Lord Himself was leading. We had no priest class, nor priest craft. These things have come in later, with the apostatizing of the movement. We did not even have a platform or pulpit in the beginning. All were on a level. The ministers were servants, according to the true meaning of the word. We did not honor men for their advantage, in means or education, but rather for their God-given "gifts." He set the members in the "body." Now "A wonderful and horrible thing is come to pass in the land. The prophets prophesy falsely, and the priests bear rule by their means; and My people love to have it so: and what will ye do in the end thereof." —Jer. 5:30, 31. Also "As for my people, children are their oppressors (sometimes grown up ones), and women rule over them." —Isa. 3:12.

Brother Seymour generally sat behind two empty shoe boxes, one on top of the other. He usually kept his head inside the top one during the meeting, in prayer. There was no pride there. The services ran almost continuously. Seeking souls could be found under the power almost any hour, night and day. The place was never closed nor empty. The people came to meet God. He was always there. Hence a continuous meeting. The meeting did not depend on the human leader. God's presence became more and more wonderful. In that old building, with its low rafters and bare floors, God took strong men and women to pieces, and put them together again, for His glory. It was a tremendous overhauling process. Pride and self-assertion, self-importance and self-esteem, could not survive there. The religious ego preached its own funeral sermon quickly.

No subjects or sermons were announced ahead of time, and no special speakers for such an hour. No one knew what might be coming, what God would do. All was spontaneous, ordered of the Spirit. We wanted to hear from God, through whoever he might speak. We had no "respect of persons." The rich and educated were the same as the poor and ignorant, and found a much harder death to die. We only recognized God. All were equal. No flesh might glory in His presence. He could not use the self-opinionated. Those were Holy Ghost meetings, led of the Lord. It had to start in poor surroundings, to keep out the selfish, human element. All came down in humility together, at His feet. They all looked alike, and had all things in common in that sense at least. The rafters were low, the tall must come down. By the time they got to "Azusa" they were humbled, ready for the blessing. The fodder was thus placed for the lambs, not for giraffes. All could reach it.

We were delivered right there from ecclesiastical hierarchism and abuse. We wanted God. When we first reached the meeting we avoided as much as possible human contact and greeting. We wanted to meet God first. We got our head under some bench in the corner in prayer, and met men only in the Spirit, knowing them "after the flesh" no more. The meetings started themselves, spontaneously, in testimony, praise and worship. The testimonies were never hurried by a call for "pop corn." We had no prearranged programme to be jammed through on time. Our time was the Lord's. We had real testimonies, from fresh heart-experience. Otherwise, the shorter the testimonies, the better. A dozen might be on their feet at one time, trembling under the mighty power of God. We did not have to get our cue from some leader. And we were free from lawlessness. We were shut up to God in prayer in the meetings, our minds on Him. All obeyed God, in meekness and humility. In honor we "preferred one another." The Lord was liable to burst through any one. We prayed for this continually. Some one would finally get up anointed for the message. All seemed to recognize this and gave way. It might be a child, a woman, or a man. It might be from the back seat, or from the front. It made no difference. We rejoiced that God was working. No one wished to show himself. We thought only of obeying God. In fact there was an atmosphere of God there that forbade any one but a fool attempting to put himself forward without the real anointing. And such did not last long. The meetings were controlled by the Spirit, from the throne. Those were truly wonderful days. I often said that **I would rather live six months at that time than fifty years of ordinary life.** But God is just the same today. Only we have changed.

Some one might be speaking. Suddenly the Spirit would fall upon the congregation. God himself would give the altar call. Men would fall all over the house, like the slain in battle, or rush for the altar enmasse, to seek God. The scene often resembled a forest of fallen trees. Such a scene cannot be imitated. I never saw an altar call given in those early days. God himself would call them. And the preacher knew when to quit. When He spoke we all obeyed. It seemed a fearful thing to hinder or grieve the Spirit. The whole place was steeped in prayer. God was in His holy temple. It was for man to keep silent. The shekinah glory rested there. In fact some claim to have seen the glory by night over the building. I do not doubt it. I have stopped more than once within two blocks of the place and prayed for strength before I dared go on. The presence of the Lord was so real.

Presumptuous men would sometimes come among us. Especially preachers who would try to spread themselves, in self-opinionation. But their effort was short lived. The breath would be taken from them. Their minds would wander, their brains reel. Things would turn black before their eyes. They could not go on. I never saw one get by with it in those days. They were up against God. No one cut them off. We simply prayed. The Holy Spirit did the rest. We wanted the Spirit to control. He wound them up in short order. They were carried out dead, spiritually speaking. They generally bit the dust in humility, going through the process we had all gone through. In other words they died out, came to see themselves in all their weakness, then in childlike humility and confession were taken up of God, transformed through the mighty "baptism" in the Spirit. The "old man" died with all his pride, arrogancy and good works. In my own case I came to abhor myself. I begged the Lord to drop a curtain so close behind me on my past that it would hit my heels. He told me to forget every good deed as though it had never occured, as soon as it was accomplished, and go forward again as though I had never accomplished anything for Him, lest my good works become a snare to me.

We saw some wonderful things in those days. Even very good men came to abhor themselves in the clearer light of God. The preachers died the hardest. They had so much to die to. So much reputation and good works. But when God got through with them they gladly turned a new page and chapter. That was one reason they fought so hard. Death is not at all a pleasant experience. And strong men die hard.

Brother Ansel Post, a Baptist preacher, was sitting on a chair in the middle of the floor one evening in the meeting. Suddenly the Spirit fell upon him. He sprang from his chair, began to praise God in a loud voice in "tongues," and ran all over the place, hugging all the brethren he could get hold of. He was filled with divine love. He later went to Egypt as a missionary. Let us have his own testimony for it: "As suddenly as on the day of Pentecost, while I was sitting some twelve feet right in front of the speaker, the Holy Spirit fell upon me and filled me literally. I seemed to be lifted up, for I was in the air in an instant, shouting "Praise God," and instantly I began to speak in another language. I could not have been more surprised if at the same moment some one had handed me a million dollars." —Ansel Post, in "Way of Faith."

After Brother Smale had invited his people back and promised them liberty in the Spirit I wrote the following, in "Way of Faith:" "The New Testament Church received her 'Pentecost" yesterday. We had a wonderful time. Men and women were prostrate under the power all over the hall. A heavenly atmosphere pervaded the place. Such singing I have never heard before, the very melody of Heaven. It seemed to come direct from the throne." —June 22, 1906.

In the "Christian Harvester" I wrote, at the same date: "At the New Testament Church a young lady of refinement was prostrate on the floor for hours, while at times the most heavenly singing would issue from her lips. It would swell away up to the throne, and then die away in an almost unearthly melody.

She sang, 'Praise God! Praise God!' All over the house men and women were weeping. A preacher was flat on his face on the floor, dying out. 'Pentecost' has fully come."

We had several all nights of prayer at the New Testament Church. But Pastor Smale never received the "baptism" with the "speaking in tongues." He was in a trying position. It was all new to him. Then the devil did his worst, to bring the work into disrepute and destroy it. He sent wicked spirits among us to frighten the pastor and cause him to reject it.

But Brother Smale was God's Moses, to lead the people as far as the Jordan, though he himself never got across. Brother Seymour led them over. And yet, strange to say, Seymour himself did not speak in "tongues" until some time after "Azusa" had been opened. Many of the saints entered in before him. All who received this "baptism" spoke in "tongues."

Many were stumbled in the beginning at "Azusa" because of the nature of the instruments first used. I wrote in "Way of Faith" as follows: "Some one has said it is not the man who can build the biggest brush heap, but rather the one who can set his heap on fire, that will light up the country. God can never wait for a perfect instrument to appear. If so He would certainly be waiting yet. Luther himself declared he was but a rough woods man, to fell the trees. Pioneers are of that nature. God has polished Melancthons, to follow up and trim and shape the timber symmetrically. A charge of dynamite does not produce the finished product. But it does set loose the stones that later stand as monuments, under the sculptor's skilled hand. Many high dignitaries of the Roman church in Luther's time were convinced of the need of a reformation, and that he was on the right track. But they declared, in so many words, that they could never consent that this new doctrine should issue from "such a corner." That it should be a monk, a poor monk, who presumes to reform us all, said they, is what we cannot tolerate. "Can any good thing come out of Nazareth?"

Fallen humanity is such a peculiar thing at its best, so shattered that it is very imperfect. "We have this treasure in earthen vessels." In the embryotic stage of all new experiences much allowance must be made for human frailty. There are always many coarse, impulsive, imperfectly balanced spirits among those first reached by a revival, also. Then our understanding of the Spirit of God is so limited that we are liable to make a mistake sometimes, failing to recognize all that may be really of God. We can understand fully only in the measure that we ourselves possess the Spirit. Snap judgment is always dangerous. "Judge nothing before the time." The company used at "Azusa" mission, to break through, were the "Gideon's band" that opened the way to victory for those to follow.

I wrote further in "Way of Faith," August 1, 1906: "Pentecost" has come to Los Angeles, the American Jerusalem. Every sect, creed, and doctrine under Heaven is found in Los Angeles, as well as every nation represented. Many times I have been tempted to wonder if my strength would hold out to see it. The burden of prayer has been very great. But since the spring of 1905, when I first received this vision and burden, I have never doubted the final outcome of it. Men are now in trouble of soul everywhere, and the revival with its unusual phenomena is the topic of the day. There is terrible opposition manifested also. The newspapers here are very venomous, and most unfair and untrue in their statements. The pseudo systems of religion are fighting hard also. But, 'the hail shall sweep away the refuge of lies.' Their 'hiding places' are being uncovered. A cleansing stream is flowing through the city. The Word of God prevails.

"Persecution is strong. Already the police have been appealed to to break up the meetings. The work has been hindered much also by fanatical spirits, of which the city has far too many. It is God and the devil for it, a battle royal. We can do little but look on and pray. The Holy Spirit Himself is taking the lead, setting aside all human leadership largely. And woe to the man who gets in His way, selfishly seeking to dictate or control. The Spirit brooks no interference of this kind. The human instruments are largely lost sight of. Our hearts and minds are directed to the Lord. The meetings are crowded out. There is great excitement among the unspiritual and unsaved.

"Every false religion under Heaven is found represented here. Next to old Jerusalem there is nothing like it in the world. (It is on the opposite side, near half way around, with natural conditions very similar also.) All nations are represented, as at Jerusalem. Thousands are here from all over the Union, and from many parts of the world, sent of God for 'Pentecost.' These will scatter the fire to the ends of the earth. Missionary zeal is at white heat. The 'gifts' of the Spirit are being given, the church's panoply restored. Surely we are in the days of restoration, the 'last days,' wonderful days, glorious days. But awful days for the withstanders. They are days of privilege, responsibility, and peril.

"Demons are being cast out, the sick healed, many blessedly saved, restored, and baptized with the Holy Ghost and power. Heroes are being developed, the weak made strong in the Lord. Men's hearts are being searched as with a lighted candle. It is a tremendous sifting time, not only of actions, but of inner, secret motives. Nothing can escape the all-searching eye of God. Jesus is being lifted up, the 'blood' magnified, and the Holy Spirit honored once more. There is much 'slaying power' manifest. And this is the chief cause of resistance on the part of those who refuse to obey. It is real business. God is with us in great earnestness. We dare not trifle. Strong men lie for hours under the mighty power of God, cut down like grass. The revival will be a world-wide one, without doubt." —F. Bartleman in "Way of Faith," August, 1906. Some time later, the pastor of the Trinity Church, M. E. South, of Los Angeles, uttered the following words: "Here on the Pacific Coast, where the sons of men meet from every quarter of the globe, prophetic souls believe the greatest moral and spiritual battles are to be fought—the Armageddon of the world."

Evan Roberts' "Message to the Churches," was voiced by him in the fallowing lines of an old poem: "While the fire of God is falling, while the voice of God is calling, brothers, get the flame. While the torch of God is burning, men's weak efforts overturning, Christians get the flame. While the Holy Ghost is pleading, human methods superseding, He himself the flame. While the power hard hearts is bending, yield thy own, to Him surrendering, all to get the flame. For the world at last is waking, and beneath His spell is breaking, into living flame. And our glorious Lord is seeking, human hearts, to rouse the sleeping, fired with heavenly flame. If in utter self-surrender, you would work with Christ, remember, you must get the flame. For the sake of bruised and dying, and the lost in darkness lying, we must get the flame. For the sake of Christ in glory, and the spreading of the story, we must get the flame. Oh, my soul, for thy refining, and thy clearer, brighter shining, do not miss the flame. On the Holy Ghost relying, simply trusting and not trying, you will get the flame. Brothers, let us cease our dreaming, and while God's flood-tide is streaming, we will have the flame."

I wrote a little tract in June, 1906, of which the following are extracts: "Opportunity once passed, is lost forever. There is a time when the tide is sweeping by our door. We may then plunge in and be carried to glorious blessing, success and victory. To stand shivering on the bank, timid, or paralyzed with stupor, at such a time, is to miss all, and most miserably fail, both for time and for eternity. Oh, our responsibility! The mighty tide of God's grace and favor is even now sweeping by us, in its prayer-directed course. There is a river (of salvation) the streams whereof make glad the city of God. —Ps. 46:4. It is time to 'get together,' and plunge in, individually and collectively. We are baptized 'in one Spirit, into one body.' —1 Cor. 12:13. Let us lay aside all carnal contentions and divisions, that separate us from each other and from God. If we are of His body, we are 'one body.' The opportunity of a lifetime, of centuries, is at our door to be eternally gained or lost. There is no time to hesitate. Act quickly, lest another take thy crown. Oh, church of Christ, awake! Be baptized with power. Then fly to rescue others. And to meet your Lord." —F. Bartleman.

"If anti-Christ is about to make his mightiest and most malignant demonstration, ought not the church to confront him with mighty displays of the Spirit's saving power?" —Gordon.

A. B. Simpson said: "We are to witness before the Lord's return real missionary "tongues" like those of Pentecost, through which the heathen world shall hear in their own language 'the wonderful works of God,' and this perhaps on a scale of whose vastness we have scarcely dreamed, thousands of missionaries going forth in one last mighty crusade from a united body of believers at home to bear swift witness of the crucified and coming Lord to all nations."

Arthur T. Pierson has said: "The most alarming peril of today is naturalism—the denial of all direct divine agency and control. Science is uniting with unbelief, wickedness and worldliness, skepticism and materialism, to rule a personal God out of the universe. This drift toward materialism and naturalism demands the supernatural as its only corrective. In Enoch's time human sin was fast making atheists, and God 'took him,' spirit, soul, and body, that men might be startled with the proof of a Divine Being, and an invisible world. In Elijah's day, general apostasy was rebuked by the descent of horses and chariots of fire; and if ever men needed to be confronted with fruits of power above nature—a living God back of all the forces and machinery He controls, who does answer prayer, guide by His providences, and convert by His grace, it is now." Oh, our weakness! Oh, our unbelief! May the Lord help us back to Pentecostal experiences. "When the Son of Man cometh, shall He find faith on the earth?"

"The presence of God in the church will put an end to infidelity. Men will not doubt His Word when they feel His Spirit. For a thousand reasons we need that Jehovah should come into the camp, as aforetimes He visited and delivered His people from bondage in Egypt." —Spurgeon's Dying Appeal.

CHAPTER 4

≈

Eighth and Maple Meetings

August 8, 1906, I rented a church building at the corner of Eighth and Maple streets, for a Pentecostal Mission. I was led to this church in February. It was then occupied by the "Pillar of Fire" people, of which Mrs. Alma White of Denver was leader. I had been impressed to pray for a building for services, after I found the New Testament Church not going ahead. But I had not known even of the existence of this building until the Lord brought me in contact with it one day, all unexpectedly. I was passing by, and saw it for the first time. I noticed it was out of regular use. It had been a German church. Through curiosity I opened the door, which was unlocked, and entered. I found the "Pillar of Fire" had it. Kneeling at the altar for a season of prayer, the Lord spoke to me. I received a wonderful witness of the Spirit. In a moment I was walking the aisles, claiming it for "Pentecost." Over the door was a large motto painted, "Gott ist die Liebe" (God is Love). This was two months before the "Azusa" work began.

I looked no further for a building, knowing that God had spoken, but waited His time. One night, six months later, in August, I was passing that way, going home from meeting, when I saw a sign, "For Rent," on the church. It had just been vacated. The Lord spoke to me: "There is your church." The "Pillar of Fire" had gone up in smoke, not able to raise the rent. They had been the most bitter opposers of the "Azusa" work. The Lord had vacated the building for us. The next day I was led to tell our landlord, Brother Fred Shepard, of the situation. I did not ask him to help me. But the Lord had sent me to him. He asked how much the rent was, went into another room, and returned quickly with a check for fifty dollars, the first month's rent. I secured the place at once.

I had another attack of stomach trouble at this time. I could scarcely eat for days, and suffered terribly. But God finally delivered. The devil tried to kill me.

I visited the M. E. camp meeting at Huntington Park to give out some revival tracts and they chased me off the grounds. One preacher threatened to knock me down. He was very zealous. I had made no trouble, only they were afraid of heresy.

The truth must be told. "Azusa" began to fail the Lord also, early in her history. God showed me one day that they were going to organize, though not a word had been said in my hearing about it. The Spirit revealed it to me. He had me get up and warn them against making a "party" spirit of the Pentecostal work. The "baptized" saints were to remain "one body," even as they had been called, and to be free as His Spirit was free, not "entangled again in a yoke of (ecclesiastical) bondage." The New Testament Church saints had already arrested their further progress in this way. God wanted a revival company, a channel through whom He could evangelize the world, blessing all people and believers. He could naturally not accomplish this with a sectarian party. That spirit has been the curse and death of every revival body sooner or later. History repeats itself in this matter.

Sure enough the very next day after I dropped this warning in the meeting I found a sign outside "Azusa" reading "Apostolic Faith Mission." The Lord said: "That is what I told you." They had done it. Surely a "party spirit" cannot be "Pentecostal." There can be no divisions in a true Pentecost. To formulate a separate body is but to advertise our failure, as a people of God. It proves to the world that we cannot get along together, rather than causing them to believe in our salvation. "That they may all be one; that the world may believe." —John 17:21. And from that time the trouble and division began. It was no longer a free Spirit for all as it had been. The work had become one more rival party and body, along with the other churches and sects of the city. No wonder the opposition steadily increased from the churches. We had been called to bless and serve the whole "body of Christ," everywhere. Christ is one, and His "body" can be but "one." To divide it is but to destroy it, as with the natural body. "In one Spirit were we all baptized into one body." —1 Cor. 12:13. The church is an organism not a human organization.

They later tried to pull the work on the whole coast into this organization, but miserably failed. The work had spread as far as Portland and Seattle, under Sister Crawford. God's people must be free from hierarchism. They are "blood-bought," and not their own. An earlier work in Texas, later tried to gather in the Pentecostal missions on the Pacific Coast, and Los Angeles, but also failed. Why should they claim authority over us? We had prayed down our own revival. The revival in California was unique and separate as to origin. It came from Heaven, even Brother Seymour not receiving the "baptism" until many others had entered in here. He did not arrive in Los Angeles until the "eleventh hour." The great battle from the beginning, both in

Los Angeles and elsewhere, has been the conflict between the "flesh" and the Spirit, between Ishmael and Isaac.

Sunday, August 12, we opened up at Eighth and Maple streets. The Spirit was mightily manifest from the very first meeting. He was given complete control. The atmosphere was terrible for sinners and backsliders. One had to get right in order to remain at Eighth and Maple. "Fearfulness" truly "surprised the hypocrites." For some days we could do little but lay before the Lord in prayer. Sister Hopkinson was a great help to me in the beginning.

The atmosphere was almost too sacred and holy to attempt to minister in. Like the priests in the Tabernacle of old we could not minister for the glory. We had terrible battles with fleshly professors and deceivers also. But God gave victory. The Spirit was much grieved by contentious spirits. The atmosphere at Eighth and Maple was for a time even deeper than at "Azusa." God came so wonderfully near us the very atmosphere of Heaven seemed to surround us. Such a divine "weight of glory" was upon us we could only lie on our faces. For a long time we could hardly remain seated even. All would be on their faces on the floor, sometimes during the whole service. I was seldom able to keep from lying full length on the floor on my face. There was a little raise of about a foot, for a platform, when we moved into the church. On this I generally lay, while God ran the meetings. They were His meetings. Every night the power of God was powerfully with us. It was glorious. The Lord seemed almost visible, He was so real. We had the greatest trouble with strange preachers, who wanted to preach. Of all the people they seemed to have the least sense. They did not know enough to keep still before Him. They liked to hear themselves. But many a preacher died in these meetings. The city was full of them, just as today. They rattled like a last year's bean pod. We had a regular " dry bone" yard. We always recognized "Azusa" as having been the mother mission, and there was never any friction or jealousy between us. We visited back and forth. Brother Seymour often met with us.

I wrote in the "Christian Harvester" at that time, as follows: "The meetings at Eighth and Maple are marvelous. We had the greatest time yesterday that I have ever seen. All day long the power of God swept the place. The church was crowded. Terrible conviction seized the people. The Spirit ran the meeting from start to finish. There was no programme, and hardly a chance for even necessary announcements. No attempt was made to preach. A few messages were given by t h e Spirit. Everybody was free to obey God. The altar was full of seeking souls all day. There was hardly a cessation of the altar service. Souls were coming out and getting through, while the meeting swept on. Men and women lay around the altar, stretched out under the power all day. A Free Methodist preacher's wife came through to a mighty "baptism," speaking some thing like Chinese. All who received the "baptism" spoke in "tongues." There were at least six Holiness preachers, some of them gray headed, honored and trusted for fruitful service for years, seeking the "baptism" most earnestly. They simply throw up their hands in the face of this revelation from God and stop to "tarry" for their "Pentecost." The president of the Holiness Church of Southern California (Brother Roberts, a precious man), was one of the first at the altar, seeking earnestly." —F. Bartleman, Los Angeles, Sept. 10, 1906.

Again I wrote, in the same paper: "The Spirit allows little human interference in the meetings, generally passing mistakes by unnoticed, or moving them out of the way Himself. Things that ordinarily we would feel must be corrected, are often passed over, and a worse calamity averted thereby. To draw attention to them brings the spirit of fear on the saints, and they stop seeking. The Spirit is hindered from working. He moves them out of the way. There are even greater issues at stake at present. We try to keep from magnifying Satan's power. We are preaching a big Christ instead. And God is using babes. The enemy is moving hell to break up our fellowship through doctrinal differences. But we must preserve the unity of the Spirit by all means. Some things can be adjusted later. They are much less important. God will never give this work into the hands of men. If it ever gets under man's control it is done. Many would join themselves to us if they did not need 'lose their heads,' get small."

On the afternoon of August 16, at Eighth and Maple, the Spirit manifested Himself through me in "tongues." There were seven of us present at the time. It was a week day. After a time of testimony and praise, with everything quiet, I was softly walking the floor, praising God in my spirit. All at once I seemed to hear in my soul (not with my natural ears), a rich voice speaking in a language I did not know. I have later heard something similar to it in India. It seemed to ravish and fully satisfy the pent up praises in my being. In a few moments I found myself, seemingly without volition on my part, enunciating the same sounds with my own vocal organs. It was an exact continuation of the same expression that I had heard in my soul a few moments before. It seemed a perfect language. I was almost like an outside listener. I was fully yielded to God, and simply carried by His will, as on a divine stream. I could have hindered the expression but would not have done so for worlds. A Heaven of conscious bliss accompanied it. It is impossible to describe the experience accurately. It must be experienced to be appreciated. There was no effort made to speak on my part, and not the least possible struggle. The experience was most sacred, the Holy Spirit playing on my vocal cords, as on an Aeolian harp. The whole utterance was a complete surprise to me. I had never really been solicitous to speak in "tongues." Because I could not understand it with my natural mind I had rather feared it.

I had no desire at the time to even know what I was saying. It seemed a soul expression purely, outside the realm of the natural mind or understanding. I was truly "sealed in the forehead," ceasing from the works of my own natural mind fully. I wrote my experience for publication later, in the following words: "The Spirit had gradually prepared me for this culmination in my experience, both in prayer for myself, and others. I had thus drawn nigh to God, my spirit greatly subdued. A place of utter abandonment of will had been reached, in absolute consciousness of helplessness, purified from natural self-activity. This process had been cumulative. The presence of the Spirit within had been as sensitive to me as the water in the glass indicator of a steam boiler.

My mind, the last fortress of man to yield, was taken possession of by the Spirit. The waters, that had been gradually accumulating, went over my head. I was possessed of Him fully. The utterance in "tongues" was without human mixture, "as the Spirit gave utterance." —(Act 2:4). Oh, the thrill of being fully yielded to Him! My mind had always been very active. Its natural workings had caused me most of my trouble in my Christian experience. "Casting down reasonings" (marginal reading, 2 Cor. 10:5). Nothing hinders faith and the operation of the Spirit so much as the self-assertiveness of the human spirit, the wisdom, strength and self-sufficiency of the human mind. This must all be crucified, and here is where the fight comes in. We must become utterly undone, insufficient and helpless in our own consciousness, thoroughly humbled, before we can receive this possession of the Holy Spirit. We want the Holy Ghost, but the fact is He is wanting possession of us.]

In the experience of "speaking in tongues" I had reached the climax in abandonment. This opened the channel for a new ministry of the Spirit in service. From that time the Spirit began to flow through me in a new way. Messages would come, with anointings, in a way I had never known before, with a spontaneous inspiration and illumination that was truly wonderful. This was attended with convincing power. The Pentecostal baptism spells complete abandonment, possession by the Holy Ghost, of the whole man, with a spirit of instant obedience. I had known much of the power of God for service for many years before this, but I now realized a sensitiveness to the Spirit, a yieldedness, that made it possible for God to possess and work in new ways and channels, with far more powerful, direct results. I also received a new revelation of His sovereignty, both in purpose and action, such as I had never known before. I found I had often charged God with seeming lack of interest, or tardiness of action, when I should have yielded to Him, in faith, that He might be able to work through me His sovereign mighty will. I went into the dust of humility at this revelation of my own stupidity, and His sovereign care and desire. I saw that the little bit of desire I possessed for His service was only the little bit that He had been able to get to me of His great desire and interest and purpose. His word declares it. All there was of good in me, in thought or action, had come from Him. Like Hudson Taylor I now felt that He was asking me simply to go with Him to help in that which He alone had purposed and desired. I felt very small at this revelation, and my past misunderstanding. He had existed, and been working out

His eternal purpose, long before I had ever been thought of, and would be long after I would be gone.

There was no strain or contortions. No struggle in an effort to get the "baptism." With me it was simply a matter of yielding. In fact it was the opposite of struggle. There was no swelling of the throat, no "operation" to be performed on my vocal organs. I had not the slightest difficulty in speaking in "tongues." And yet I can understand how some may have such difficulties. They are not fully yielded to God. With me the battle had been long drawn out. I had already worn myself out, fully yielded. God deals with no two individuals alike. I was not really seeking the "baptism" when I got it. And in fact I never sought it as a definite experience. I wanted to be yielded fully to God. But beyond that I had no real definite expectation or desire. I wanted more of Him, that was all.

There was no shouting crowd around me, to confuse or excite me. No one was suggesting "tongues" to me at the time, either by argument or imitation. Thank God He is able to do His work without such help, and far better without it. I do not believe in dragging the child forth, spiritually speaking, with instruments. I do believe in sane, earnest prayer help in the Spirit. Too many souls are dragged from the womb of conviction by force, and have to be incubated ever after. As with nature, so in grace. It is best to dispense as far as possible with the doctors and old mid-wives. The child is almost killed at times through their unnatural violence. A pack of jackals over their prey could hardly act more fiercely than we have witnessed in some cases. In natural child birth it is generally best to let the mother alone as far as possible. We should stand by and encourage, but not force the deliverance. Natural births are better.

I had been shut up largely to a ministry of intercession and prophecy before this, until I should reach this condition of utter abandonment to the Spirit. I was now to go forth again in the service. When my day of "Pentecost" was fully come the channel was cleared. The living waters burst forth. The door of my service sprang open at the touch of the hand of a sovereign God. The Spirit began to operate within me in a new and mightier way. It was a distinct, fresh climax and development, an epochal experience for me. And for this we had been shut up as a company. The preparation was world-wide, among the saints of God. The results have already made history. In fact this has proven an epoch in the history of the church just as distinct and definite as the Spirit's action in the time of Luther and Wesley, and with far greater portend. And it is not yet all history. We are too close to it yet to understand or appreciate it fully. But we have made another step back on the way to the restoration of the church as in the beginning. We are completing the circle. Jesus will return for a perfect church, "without spot or wrinkle." He is coming for "one body," not a dozen. He is the Head, and as such He is no monstrosity, with a hundred bodies. "That they all may be one, that the world may believe." This after all is the greatest "sign" to the world. "Though we speak with the tongues of men and of angels, and have not love, etc." —1 Cor. 13. I felt after the experience of speaking in "tongues" that languages would come easy to me. And so it has proven. And also I have learned to sing, in the Spirit. I never was a singer, and do not know music.

I never sought "tongues." My natural mind resisted the idea. This phenomena necessarily violates human reason. It means abandonment of this faculty for the time. And this is generally the last point to yield. The human mind is held in abeyance fully in this exercise. And this is "foolishness," and a stone of stumbling, to the natural mind or reason. It is supernatural. We need not expect anyone who has not reached this depth of abandonment in their human spirit, this death to their own reason, to either accept or understand it. The natural reason must be yielded in the matter. There is a gulf to cross, between reason and revelation. But this principle in experience is just that which leads to the "Pentecostal" baptism, as in Acts 2:4. It is the underlying principle of the "baptism." And this is why the simple people get in first, though perhaps not always so well balanced or capable otherwise. They are like the little boys going swimming, to use a homely illustration. They get in first because they have the least clothes to divest themselves of. We must all come "naked" into this experience. All of self gone.

The early church lived in this, as its normal atmosphere. Hence its abandonment to the working of the Spirit, its supernatural "gifts," and its power. Our wiseacres cannot reach this. Oh, to become a fool, to know nothing in ourselves, that we might receive the mind of Christ fully, have the Holy Ghost teach and lead us only, and at all times. We do not mean to say we must talk in "tongues" continually. The "baptism" is not all "tongues." We can live in this place of illumination and abandonment and still speak in our own language. The Bible was not written in 'tongues." But we may surely live in the Spirit at all times, though possibly few, if any, always do. Oh, the depth of abandonment, all self gone! Conscious of knowing nothing, of having nothing, except as the Spirit shall teach and impart to us. This is the true place of power, of God's power, in the ministry of service. There is nothing left but God, the pure Spirit. Every hope or sense of capability in the natural is gone. We live by His breath, as it were. The "wind" on the day of

"Pentecost" was the breath of God. —Acts 2:2. But what more can we say? It must be experienced to be understood. It cannot be explained. We have certainly had a measure of the Spirit before without this. To this fact all history testifies. The church has been abnormal since its fall. But we cannot have the "Pentecostal" baptism without it, as the early church had it. The Apostles received it suddenly, and in full. Only simple faith and abandonment can receive it. Human reason can find all kinds of flaws and apparent foolishness in it.

I spoke in "tongues" possibly for about fifteen minutes on this first occasion. Then the immediate inspiration passed away, for the time. I have spoken at times since, also. But I never try to reproduce it. The act must be sovereign with God. It would be foolishness and sacrilege to try to imitate it. The experience left behind it the consciousness of a state of utter abandonment to the Lord, a place of perfect rest from my own works and activity of mind. It left with me a consciousness of utter God-control, and of His presence naturally in corresponding measure. It was a most sacred experience. Many have trifled most foolishly with this principle and possession. They have failed to continue in the Spirit and have stumbled many. This has wrought great harm. But the experience still remains as a fact, both in history and present day realization. The greater part of most Christians' knowledge of God is and has always been, since the loss of the Spirit by the early church, an intellectual knowledge. Their knowledge of the word and principles of God is an intellectual one, through natural reasoning and understanding largely. They have little revelation, illumination or inspiration direct from the Spirit of God.

We will quote from well known authors some interesting extracts on the subject of "speaking in tongues." Dr. Philip

Schaff, in his "History of the Christian Church," Vol. 1, page 116, says: "The speaking with tongues is an involuntary psalm—like prayer or song, uttered from a spiritual trance, and in a peculiar language inspired by the Holy Ghost. The soul is almost entirely passive, an instrument on which the Holy Ghost plays His heavenly melodies."

Conybeare and Howson, commentators, write: "This gift (speaking in tongues) was the result of a sudden influx of the supernatural to the believer. Under its influence the exercise of the understanding was suspended, while the spirit was wrapped in a state of ecstacy by the immediate communication of the Spirit of God. In this ecstatic trance the believer was constrained by irresistible power to pour forth his feelings of thanksgiving and rapture in words not his own. He was usually even ignorant of their meaning." Space forbids our quoting from other standard commentators on this subject. Many have written very illuminatingly on the same subject., and to the same general end as those we have quoted. We will quote from just one more writer.

Stalker, in his "Life of Paul," page 102, has the following to say: "It (the speaking in tongues) seems to have been a kind of tranced utterance, in which the speaker poured out an impassioned rhapsody, by which his religious faith received both expression and exaltation. Some were not able to tell others the meaning of what they were saying, while others had this additional power; and there were those who, though not speaking in tongues themselves, were able to interpret what the inspired speakers were saying. In all cases there seems to have been a kind of immediate inspiration, so that what they did was not the effect of calculation or preparation, but of a strong present impulse. These phenomena are so remarkable, that, if narrated in a history, they would put a severe strain on Christian faith. They show with what mighty force at its first entrance into the world, Christianity took possession of the spirits it touched. The very gifts of the Spirit were perverted into instruments of sin; for those possessed of the more showy gifts, such as miracles and tongues, were too fond of displaying them, and turned them into grounds of boasting." There is always more or less danger attached to privileges. Children frequently cut themselves with sharp knives. But we are certainly in more danger from remaining in stagnation, where we are, than in going ahead trustingly for God.

Describing some of my personal experiences, previous to my "baptism," I wrote the following in "Christian Harvester:" "My own heart was searched until I cried out under the added light, 'God deliver me from my religious self-consciousness!' Seldom have I suffered in humility, shame and reproach, as at this vision of my very best in the sight of God. My religious comeliness was indeed turned into corruption. I felt that I could not bear to hear, or even to think of it again. I felt I would be glad to forget even my own name and identity. I even destroyed with extreme satisfaction records of my past achievements for God, upon which my eyes had loved to linger. I now abhorred them, as a temptation from the devil to self-exaltation. Letters of commendation for religious services rendered, literary works of seeming excellence to me, and sermons which to me had seemed wonderful in knowledge and construction, now actually nauseated me, because of the element of self-pride detected in them. I found I had come to rest on these more or less for expected divine favor and reward. 'Nothing but the blood of Jesus,' had at least partially been lost sight of. I was depending on other things besides to recommend me to God. And in this lay great danger. I now destroyed these treasured documents, false evidences, as I would a viper, lest they tempt me from the efficacy of His merits alone. It meant a deep heart searching. I knew of but few Holiness leaders who were really being dealt with on this line so deeply.

"Past services now became a very blank to me, and with the greatest relief on my part. I began again for God, as though I had never accomplished anything. I felt that I stood before Him empty handed. The fire of testing seemed to sweep away all of my religious doings. God did not want me to rest in these. For the future I was to forget all that I might ever do for God, as quickly as it was accomplished, so that it might not prove a further snare to me, and go on as though I had never done a thing for God. This was my safety." Without a doubt the least satisfaction to self in one's religious service is the greatest hindrance to the blessing and favor of God. It must be shunned as we would a serpent.

We continued to have wonderful meetings at Eighth and Maple. The Lord showed me he wanted this work to go deeper yet than anything we had at that time attained to. He was not even satisfied fully with the "Azusa" work, deep as it had gone. There was still too much of the self-life, the religious self, among us. This naturally meant war, hard and bitter, from the enemy. Ours was to be a sort of "clearing station," where fleshly exercises, false manifestations, and the religious self in general should be dealt with. We were after real experience, permanent and established, with God-like character, and no relapses.

The Holiness people were especially most tenacious of their attainments and position. In fact many of them were filled with hard-hearted pharisaism. Only God could hope to get light to them on their condition and need. They had largely lost their "first love," with little left but the shell of their profession. There seemed even more hope for the church people. They were not so hard, censorious, critical and bigoted, on the whole. Our "shibboleth" may become a "brazen serpent," which we set up on a pole to worship. As such it will cease to heal us, and become a "piece of brass" (margin, 2 Kings 18:4), to be smashed.

I was greatly tested financially again. One day I had to walk twenty-five blocks to town, not having even carfare. A brother almost as poor as myself gave me a nickel to ride home. At the same time we were having glorious meetings. Many were prostrated under the power. The devil sent two strong characters one night to sidetrack the work. A spiritualist woman put herself at the head, like a drum major, to lead the singing. I prayed her out of the church. The other, a fanatical preacher with a voice that almost rattled the windows, I had to rebuke openly. He took over the whole meeting. Conceit fairly stuck out of him. The Spirit was terribly grieved. God could not work. I had suffered too much for the work to turn the whole thing over to the devil so easily. Besides I was responsible for souls, and for the rent. So I had to tell him to leave.

We had a fierce battle with such spirits. They would have ruined everything. The devil has no conscience, and the "flesh" has no sense. The very first time I opened the church for meetings I found one of the worst fanatics and religious crooks sitting on the steps waiting for me. He wanted to run the place. He was a preacher. I chased him from the place, like Nehemiah did the son of Joiada. (Neh. 13:28.) I had never dreamed there was so much of the devil in so many people. The town seemed full of them. It tempted the saints to fight and hindered the Spirit. These crooks and cranks were the first at the meeting. We had a great clearing-up time. Especially in the case of old professors. There was much professional, religious quackery. Judgment had to "begin at the house of God." Luther was greatly troubled with wilful, religious fanatics in his day. He wrote from the Wartburg, where he was then concealed, to Melancthon at Wittemberg, a test-stone for these fanatics, as follows: "Ask these prophets whether they have felt those spiritual torments, those creations of God, that death and hell which accompany a real separation." When he returned to Wittemberg and they tried their sorcery on him he met them with these crude words: "I slap your spirit on the snout." They acted like devils at that challenge. But it broke their spell.

We were obliged to deal firmly with extreme cases, but in the main the Spirit passed over and moved out of the way irregularities, without further advertising them. Many have declared we cannot throw our meetings open today. Then we must shut God out also. What we need is more of God, to control the meetings. He must be left free to come forth at all costs. The saints themselves are too largely in confusion and rebellion. Through prayer and self-abasement God will undertake for the meetings. This was the secret in the beginning. We held together in prayer, love, and unity, and no power could break this. But self must be burned out. Meetings must be controlled by way of the throne. A spiritual atmosphere must be created, through humility and prayer, that Satan cannot live in. And this we realized in the beginning. It was the very opposite of religious zeal, and carnal, religious ambition. We knew nothing about present day "pep" and "make it snappy" methods. That whole system is a bastard product, as far as "Pentecost" is concerned. It takes time to be holy. The world rushes on. It gets us nowhere with God.

One reason for the depth of the work at "Azusa" was the fact that the workers were not novices. They were largely called and prepared for years, from the Holiness ranks, and from the mission field, etc. They had been burnt out, tried and proven. They were largely seasoned veterans. They had walked with God and learned deeply of His Spirit. These were pioneers, "shock troops," the Gideon's three hundred, to spread the fire around the world. Just as the disciples had been prepared by Jesus. We have now taken on a "mixed multitude." And the seeds of apostasy have had time to work. "First love" has been also largely lost. The dog has "returned to his vomit" in many cases, to Babylonic doctrines and practices. An enfeebled mother can hardly be expected to bring forth healthy children.

The Spirit dealt so deeply, and the people were so hungry in the beginning, that the carnal, human spirit injected into the meetings seldom failed to hinder largely the working of the Spirit. It was as though a stranger had broken into a private, select company. The presence was painfully noticeable. Men were after God. He was in His holy temple, earth (the human) must keep silence before Him. It only caused grief and pain. Our so-called tarrying and prayer rooms today are but a shadow of the former ones, too often a place to blow off steam in human enthusiasm, or become mentally intoxicated, supposedly from the Holy Ghost. Many of them are a kind of lethal chamber, with very little of the pure Spirit of God. This should not be. We had a tremendous lot of fanaticism in the Holiness movement also. In the early days the "tarrying room" was the first thought and provision for a "Pentecostal Mission." It was held sacred, a kind of "holy ground." There was mutual consideration also. There men sought to become quiet from the activities of their own too active mind and spirit, to escape from the world for the time, and get alone with God. There was no noisy, wild, exciting spirit there. That at least could be done elsewhere. The claims and confusion of an exacting world were shut out. It was a sort of "city of refuge" from this sort of thing, a "haven of rest," where God could be heard, and talk to their souls. Men would spend hours in silence there, searching their own hearts in privacy, and securing the mind of the Lord for future action. This sort of thing seems well nigh impossible today amid present surroundings. We die out to self by coming into His presence. And this requires great quietness of spirit. We need a "holy of holies." What Jew of old would have dared to act in God's temple as we do today in the missions? It would have meant death to him. We are full of foolishness and fanatical self-assertion. Even the formal Romanists have more reverence on the whole than we.

Sunday, August 26, Pastor Pendleton and about forty of his members came into Eighth and Maple, to worship with us. They had received the "baptism" and spoken in "tongues" in their church. The Holiness Church had thrown them out of their own building for this, to them, unpardonable crime. This congregation had built a church with their own money. The property was worth ten thousand dollars. But they gladly left it to follow Jesus. It had been deeded to the Association. This would seem to be a great mistake in such cases. The property should belong to the local assembly. I had been impressed to say to Brother Pendleton some weeks before this, when meeting him at "Azusa," that I believed we would yet worship together. This was even before I had gotten Eighth and Maple. I had no meeting of my own at that time. But the impression proved to have been from the Lord. At that time he was not thinking of ever needing another place to worship. He had not yet received the "baptism." When I heard the church was going to try him for heresy I invited them to come in with us if they were thrown out. Two days later they were expelled, and accepted my invitation. They came in in a body. I had been praying for just such help as I was by this time very much worn in body.

Tradition is a tremendous curse in its power for thralldom. The Holiness church doubtless verily believed that Brother Pendleton and his flock had gone radically astray. They had no better pastor nor members in their connection. Brother Pendleton declared after this experience that he would never build another doctrinal roof over his head. He was determined to go on for God. Multitudes are shut up in ecclesiastical systems, within sectarian boundaries, while God's great, free pasture lies out before them, only limited by the encircling Word of God. "There shall be one flock, and one Shepherd." —(See Ps. 23.) Traditional theology, partial truth and revelation, soon becomes law. The conscience is utterly bound, like Chinese foot-binding, shut up against further progress.

I first met Brother Daniel Awrey here at Eighth and Maple. He came to the meetings and we had a laughing blessing together. I was with him later in India and China. He finally died in Africa. We were tremendously burdened for souls in those days, and had many all nights of prayer at the church. It seemed an easy thing to remain in prayer all night. It generally became daylight almost before we could realize it. We did not get sleepy. We had entered into the life of eternity, where there is no time. The presence of the Lord was wonderfully real. Sometimes the night seemed not more than half an hour, we were so quickened and exhilirated by the Spirit.

Sunday, September 9, was a wonderful day. Several were stretched out under the power for hours. The altar was full all day, with scarcely any cessation to the services. Several received the "baptism." In those days we preached but little. The people were taken up with God. Brother Pendleton and myself could generally be found lying full length on the low platform on our faces, in prayer, during the services. It was almost impossible to stay off our faces in those days. The presence of the Lord was so real. And this condition lasted for a long time. We had but little to do with guiding the meetings. Everyone was looking to God alone. We felt almost like apologizing when we had to claim any attention from the people, for announcements. It was a continuous sweep of victory. God had their attention. The audience would be at times convulsed with penitence. God dealt deeply with sin in those days. It could not remain in the camp.

At times my prayers were wonderfully answered for finances. I needed ten dollars for our house rent, and five dollars to pay for tracts. The owner cancelled the month's house rent, without a word from me. Then a sister handed me a sealed envelope. I opened it and found just five dollars in it. I had not said a word about my needs.

The New Testament Church had a split about this time. I was glad I had nothing to do with that. Brother Smale had forced the "baptized" saints to the wall. He had rejected their testimony finally. Brother Elmer Fisher then started another mission at 327 ½ South Spring street, known as the "Upper Room" mission. Most of the white saints from "Azusa" went with him, with the "baptized" ones from the New Testament Church. This later became for a time the strongest mission in town. Both "Azusa" and the New Testament Church had by this time largely failed God. I soon after turned Eighth and Maple over to Brother Pendleton, as I was too worn to continue longer in constant service in the meetings. I had been for a long time under constant strain in prayer and meetings, and needed a rest and change very badly.

In the beginning of the "Pentecostal" work I became very much exercised in the Spirit that Jesus should not be slighted, "lost in the temple," by the exaltation of the Holy Ghost, and of the "gifts" of the Spirit. There seemed great danger of losing sight of the fact that Jesus was "all, and in all." I endeavored to keep Him as the central theme and figure before the people. Jesus should be the center of our preaching. All comes through and in Him. The Holy Ghost is given to "show the things of Christ." The work of Calvary, the atonement, must be the center for our consideration. The Holy Ghost never draws our attention from Christ to Himself, but rather reveals Christ in a fuller way. We are in the same danger today. There is nothing deeper nor higher than to know Christ. Everything is given of God to that end. The "one Spirit" is given to that end. Christ is our salvation, and our all. That we might know "the lengths and breadths, and heights and depths of the love of Christ, having a "spirit of wisdom and revelation in the knowledge of Him (Christ)." —Eph. 1:17. It was "to know Him (Christ)," for which Paul strove. I was led to suddenly present Jesus one night to the congregation at Eighth and Maple. They had been forgetting Him in their exaltation of the Holy Ghost and the "gifts." Now I introduced Christ for their consideration. They were taken completely by surprise and convicted in a moment. God made me do it. Then they saw their mistake and danger. I was preaching Christ one night at this time, setting Him before them in His proper place, when the Spirit so witnessed of His pleasure that I was overpowered by His presence, falling helpless to the floor under a mighty revelation of Jesus to my soul. I fell like John on the Isle of Patmos, at His feet.

I wrote a tract at this time, of which the following are extracts: "We may not even hold a doctrine, or seek an experience, except in Christ. Many are willing to seek "power" from every battery they can lay their hands on, in order to perform miracles, draw the attention and adoration of the people to themselves, thus robbing Christ of His glory, and making a fair showing in the flesh. The greatest religious need of our day would seem to be that of true followers of the meek and lowly Jesus. Religious enthusiasm easily goes to seed. The human spirit so predominates, the show-off, religious spirit. But we must stick to our text, Christ. He alone can save. The attention of the people must be first of all, and always, held to Him. A true "Pentecost" will produce a mighty conviction for sin, a turning to God. False manifestations produce only excitement and wonder. Sin and self-life will not materially suffer from these. We must get what our conviction calls for. Believe in your own heart's hunger, and go ahead with God. Don't allow the devil to rob you of a real "Pentecost." Any work that exalts the Holy Ghost or the "gifts" above Jesus will finally land up in fanaticism. Whatever causes us to exalt and love Jesus is well and safe. The reverse will ruin all. The Holy Ghost is a great light, but focused on Jesus always, for His revealing.

A. S. Worrell, translator of the New Testament, was an earnest friend of "Pentecost," and a seeker after the "baptism." He wrote the following in the "Way of Faith:" "The blood of Jesus is exalted in these meetings as I have rarely known elsewhere. There is a mighty power manifest in witnessing for Jesus, with a wonderful love for souls. There is also a bestowal of 'gifts of the Spirit.' The places of meeting are at Azusa street, at the New Testament Church, where Joseph Smale is pastor; some of his people were among the first to speak with 'tongues,' but most have withdrawn because they felt restraint in his church; and at Eighth and Maple streets, where Pastors Bartleman and Pendleton are the principal leaders."

In September, 1906, the following letters appeared in the "Way of Faith," from the pen of Dr. W. C. Dumble, of Toronto, Canada, who was visiting Los Angeles at this time. But, first, a note from Editor Pike himself. He wrote: "For some months we have been receiving letters from our dear Brother Bartleman concerning the great work of the Holy Spirit in Los Angeles. There has been some criticism of the reports we have published, and we were just on the point of writing to others on the ground, when our dear brother, Dr. W. C. Dumble, favored us with the following most interesting description of what he has seen and felt there." The following from Dr. Dumble: "Possibly some of your readers may be interested in the impressions of a stranger in Los Angeles. A similar gracious work of the Spirit to that in Wales is in progress here. But while that is mostly in the churches, this is outside. The churches will not have it, or up to the present have stood aloof in a critical and condemnatory spirit. Like the work in Wales, this is a laymen's revival conducted by the Holy Spirit, and carried on in halls, and old tumble-down buildings, such as can be gotten for the work.

"This is a remarkable movement, that may be said to be peculiar by the appearance of the 'gift of tongues.' There are three different missions where one may hear these strange tongues. I had the rare joy of spending last evening at Pastor Bartleman's meeting, or more correctly at a meeting where he and Pastor Pendleton are the nominal leaders, but where the Holy Spirit is actually in control. Jesus is proclaimed the Head, and the Holy Ghost His executive. Hence there is no preaching, no choir, no organ, no collection, except what is voluntarily placed on the table, or put in the box on the wall. And God was mightily present last night. Some one begins to sing: three or four hymns may be sung, interspersed with hallelujahs and amens. Then some overburdened soul rises, and shouts, 'Glory to Jesus!' and amid sobs and tears tells of a great struggle, and a great deliverance. Then three or four are on the floor with shining faces. One begins to praise God, and then breaks out with uplifted hands into a 'tongue.' Pastor Pendleton now tells how he felt the need, and sought the 'baptism,' and God baptized him with such an experience of the divine presence and love and boldness as he had never had before. The officials of his church therefore desired him to withdraw, and a number of his people went with him and joined forces with Pastor Bartleman. Then a sweet faced old German Lutheran lady told how she wondered when she heard the people praising God in 'tongues,' and began to pray to be baptized with the Spirit. After she had gone to bed her mouth went off in a 'tongue,' and she praised the Lord through the night to the amazement of her children.

"Next an exhortation in 'tongues' comes from Pastor Bartleman's lips in great sweetness, and one after another make their way to the altar quickly, until the rail is filled with seekers. Whatever criticism may be offered to this work it is very evident that it is divinely endorsed, and the Lord is 'adding to them daily such as are being saved.' It is believed that this revival is but in its infancy, and the assurance has been given that a great outpouring is imminent, and that we are in the evening of this dispensation. The burden of the 'tongues' is, 'Jesus is coming soon.'" —W. C. Dumble, Los Angeles, Calif., Sept. 6, 1906.

Dr. Dumble wrote again, for the same paper: "At Pastor Bartleman's church meetings are held every night, all day Sundays, and all night every Friday. There is no order of services, they are expected to run in the divine order. The blessed Holy Ghost is the executive in charge. The leaders, or pastors, will be seen most of the time on their faces on the floor, or kneeling in the place where the pulpit commonly is, but there is neither pulpit, nor organ, nor choir. A young lady, for the first time in one of these meetings, came under the power of the Spirit, and lay for half an hour with beaming face lost to all about her, beholding visions unutterable. Soon she began to say, 'Glory! Glory to Jesus!' and spoke fluently in a strange tongue. On Sabbath last the meeting continued from early morning to midnight. There was no preaching, but prayer, testimony, praise, and exhortation." —W. C. Dumble. Much more of interest was contained in these published letters, but space forbids.

It is a fact that in the beginning platforms and pulpits were as far as possible removed out of the way. We had no conscious need of them. Priest class and ecclesiastical abuse were entirely swept away. We were all "brethren." All were free to obey God. He might speak through whom He would. He had poured out His Spirit "on all flesh," even on His servants and hand maidens. —Act. 2. We honored men for their God-given "gifts" and offices only. As the movement began to apostatize platforms were built higher, coat tails were worn longer, choirs were organized, and string bands came into existence to "jazz" the people. The kings came back once more, to their thrones, restored to sovereignty. We were no longer "brethren." Then the divisions multiplied, etc. While Brother Seymour kept his head inside the old empty box in "Azusa" all was well. They later built for him a throne also. Now we have, not one hierarchy, but many. ("Azusa Mission" is deserted, and Brother Seymour is in Heaven at this writing.) Kipling's immortal poem might well be recollected here: "The tumult and the shouting dies;

the captains and the kings depart: Still stands thine ancient sacrifice, an humble and a contrite heart." God will not have us worship men or places.

I wrote for another religious paper the following, in 1906: "Cursed with unbelief we are struggling upward, only with the utmost difficulty, for the restoration of that glorious light and power, once so bountifully bestowed on the church, but long since lost. Our eyes have been so long blinded by the darkness of unbelief into which we were plunged by the church's fall, that we fight the light, for our eyes are weak. So far had we fallen as a church that when Luther sought to restore the truth of 'justi-fication by faith' it was fought and resisted by the church of his day as the utmost heresy, and men paid for it with their lives. And it was much the same in Wesley's time. But here we are with the restoration of the very experience of 'Pentecost,' with the 'latter rain,' a restoration of the power, in greater glory, to finish up the work begun. We shall again be lifted to the church's former level, to complete her work, begin where they left off when failure overtook them, and speedily fulfilling the last great commission, open the way for the coming of the Christ.

"We are to drop out the centuries of the church's failure, the long, dismal 'dark ages,' and telescoping time be now fully restored to pristine power, victory and glory. We seek to pull ourselves, by the grace of God, out of a corrupt, backslidden, spurious Christianity. The synagogues of a proud, hypocritical church are arrayed against us, to give us the lie. The 'hirelings' thirst for our blood. The scribes and pharisees, chief priests, and rulers of the synagogues, are all against us and the Christ.

"Los Angeles seems to be the place, and this the time, in the mind of God, for the restoration of the church to her former place, favor and power. The fulness of time seems to have come for the church's complete restoration. God has spoken to His servants in all parts of the world, and has sent many of them to Los Angeles, representing every nation under Heaven once more, as of old, come up for 'Pentecost,' to go out again into all the world with the glad message of salvation. The base of operations has been shifted, from old Jerusalem, for the latter 'Pentecost,' to Los Angeles. And there is a tremendous, God-given hunger for this experience everywhere. Wales was but intended as the cradle for this world-wide restoration of the power of God. India but the Nazareth where He was 'brought up.'" —F. Bartleman, Oct., 1906, in "Apostolic Light."

Again I wrote in the same paper: "If ever men shall seek to control, corner or own this work of God, either for their own glory or for that of a organization we shall find the Spirit refusing to work. The glory will depart. Let this be one work where God shall be given His proper place, and we shall see such a work as men have never yet dreamed of. It would be a fearful thing if God were obliged to withdraw His blessed Spirit from us, or withold it at such a time as this, because we tried to corner it. All our business is to get God to the people. Let us yield ourselves for this, and this alone. Some of the 'canker worms' of past experience have been party spirit, sectional difference; prejudices, etc., which are all carnal, contrary and destructive to the law of love, to the 'one body' of Christ. 'For in one Spirit are we all baptized into one body.' —1 Cor. 12: 13. Self-satisfaction will always cause defeat. Oh, brother! cease traveling 'round and 'round your old habit-beaten path, on which all grass has ceased to grow, and strike out into pastures green, beside the living waters." —F. Bartleman, Dec., 1906.

In the "Way of Faith" I wrote the following: "We are coming back from the 'dark ages' of the church's backsliding and downfall. We are living in the most momentous moments of the history of time. The Spirit is brushing aside all our plans, our schemes, our strivings, and our theories, and is Himself acting again. Many who have feathered well their nests are fighting hard. They cannot sacrifice to rise to these conditions.

"The precious ore of truth, the church's emancipation from the thralldom of man's rule, has been brought about in a necessarily crude form at first, as rough ore. It has been surrounded, as in nature, by all kinds of worthless, hurtful elements. Extravagant, violent characters have sought to identify themselves with the work. A monster truth is struggling in the bowels of the earth, entombed by the landslide of retrograding evil in the church's history. But it is bursting forth, soon to shake itself free from the objectionable matter yet clinging to it, unavoidably for the time. Christ is at last proclaimed the Head. The Holy Spirit is the life. The members are in principle all 'one body.' " —F. Bartleman, Dec., 1906.

Again, some extracts from an article in the "Way of Faith: "We detect in the present hour manifestations in our midst the rising of a new order of things out of the chaos and failure of the past. The atmosphere is filled with inspiring expectation of the ideal. But unbelief retards our progress. Our preconceived ideas betray us in the face of opportunity. They lead to loss and ruin. But the world is awakening today, startled from her guilty slumber of ease and death. Letters are pouring in from every side, from all parts of the world, inquiring feverishly, 'what meaneth this?' Ah, we have the pulse of humanity, especially of the church of today. There is a mighty expectation. And these hungry, expectant children are crying for bread. Cold, intellectual speculation has had nothing but denials for them. The realm of the Spirit cannot be reached alone by the intellect.

The miraculous has again startled us into a realization of the fact that God still lives, and moves among us.

"Old forms are breaking up, passing away. Their death knell is being sounded. New forms, a new order and life, are appearing. There is naturally a mighty struggle. Satan moves the hosts of hell to hinder. But we shall conquer. The precious ore must be refined after it has been mined. The 'precious' must be taken 'from the vile.' Rough pioneers have cleared the way for our advance, through the thick underbrush. Heroic, positive spirits are necessary for this work. But purer forms will follow.

"Men have been speaking adown the ages, but the voice of God the Spirit is calling us today. Since the early church lost her power and place with God we have been struggling back. Up through 'its' and 'isms,' theories, creeds and doctrines (and schisms), issues and movements, blessings and experiences and professions, we have come. The stream could rise no higher than its source. We need no more theology or theory. Let the devil have them. Let us get to God. Many are cramped up in present experiences. **They are actually afraid to seek more of God for fear the devil will get them.** Away with such foolish bondage! Follow your heart! **Believe in your own heart's hunger, and go ahead for God.** We are sticking to the bottom. We need the fire of God. Straight-jacket methods and religious rules have well nigh crushed out our spiritual life altogether. We had better grieve all men rather than God." —F. Bartleman, Jan., 1907.

Before the "Azusa" outpouring everything had settled down in concrete form, bound by man. Nothing could move for God. Dynamite, the power of the Holy Ghost, was necessary to free this mass. And this God furnished. The whole mass was set free once more. Our "year of Jubilee" had come. The last one had been realized in the great revival of '59, fifty years before.

The house we were living in was sold and we were obliged to move. I went to see some rooms and they looked so nice and large I took them at once. It was God's place for us, at 1319 San Pedro street. But I had a strange experience in this connection. I hardly knew them when we moved in. They looked so much smaller. It had been a divine "optical illusion," by the Spirit. But He made us satisfied. We had been so nicely situated before it was a great change. The owner lived in one side of the house and was very wicked. We had a single, partnership aisle between, with a "slot" gas meter for both parties. We had much trouble as to whose turn it was to drop in the quarter. But the Lord kept us sweet. The owner drank and caroused much. We suspicioned her of being immoral also. She was a widow, with a family. She had male callers. It required much grace to remain there. But it was God's choice for us at the time.

Our church landlord, a Jew, now raised the rent on us. He evidently thought we were too prosperous. I was so worn by this time, from prayer and constant meetings, that I turned the pastorate over to Brother Pendleton fully. He had been a pastor before. I then began to stay at home more to rest and recuperate. I had written much, attended meetings constantly, besides going through the terrific siege of prayer both before and after the outpouring, so that my nerves were completely exhausted. I could hardly contemplate the writing of an ordinary postcard without mental agony at this time. I now decided to give myself to prayer, the study of the Word, and evangelistic work, as the Lord should lead. I had been tied to the Eighth and Maple meetings night and day. I can sympathize with Evan Roberts' nervous breakdown, after the revival in Wales. Eighth and Maple meetings ran for years after this, as a free mission. We never gave it a name. God marvelously used it. Dr. Yoakum held meetings there for a long time, in connection with Pastor Pendleton. Hundreds of souls were saved and blessed there. Brother Pendleton finally died, the lot was sold, and the building torn down. Only Heaven will reveal the good done and the soul and bodies blessed at Eighth and Maple. I want to repeat again there was never any jealousy or rivalry between Eighth and Maple Mission and "Azusa." God saved us from that spirit. It would have robbed us of His blessing. Brother Seymour always declared I had a company of angels traveling with me.

I spent whole nights in prayer, which did not seem a hardship but a privilege. The Lord was so near. I also wrote a number of new tracts, though very weak in body. My spirit could not rest from constant service. The message was upon me. Traditional teaching was so deep rooted in the people the Spirit strove constantly to free them, through this tract ministry.

"We should bring all human opinions and maxims to the Scriptures, as to a touchstone, by which to try them." —Luther. Luther himself suffered Gethsemanes of agony in breaking away from the Roman traditions. It is like death to break away from that which has become a very part of our religious being. Tradition becomes as binding upon us as the Word of God itself, and has become accepted as the same. And yet how much tradition has been proven all wrong scripturally.

I went to Santa Barbara for a change, preaching at the "Faith Mission," and at the Holiness Church there. I then spent a Sunday with Brother Harry Morse, in the Peniel Mission at San Pedro. Had a blessed time preaching. My time was mostly divided between meetings at Eighth and Maple, "Azusa" mission, Pasadena and Hermon. I frequently visited the "Upper Room" mission, 327½ South Spring street, also. We came into severe testings in January. I had no money and we were almost out of food. Then the devil attacked me with a terrible stomach neuralgia. I cried to the Lord in desperation, as I was suffering horribly. He touched and relieved me at once of the pain, and I was also able to go to meeting and give Him glory.

The missions were drifting into the hands of man again and much "flesh" at times was manifest. I tried to keep true to the "heavenly vision." At times the manifestations would become of such a character there seemed little Spirit in them. They would evaporate into thin air. At other times the meetings were very powerful. But the temptation seemed to be always, as today, toward empty manifestation. This does not require any particular cross, or death to the self-life. Hence it is always popular. But there is only one safe, honest course to pursue with the "old man." Bury him under six feet of earth, with his face downward. The harder he scratches the deeper he will go.

I went to San Pedro again, and preached at Peniel Mission on Acts 2:4. While I was "yet preaching" the Spirit fell. We went immediately to prayer and had a wonderful time. At Hermon I preached a number of times.

God had given me a wonderful tract ministry. In two years' time I had published, by faith purely, without a dollar to begin with, fifty-eight separate tracts. About fifty of these I had written myself. I circulated two hundred and fifty thousand, at a cost of at least five hundred dollars. No money was solicited, and thousands were mailed free to all parts of the world also. I ended the ministry without a dollar. No money had been made out of it.

One evening at this time I went to the little Alley Mission in Pasadena. I had a heavy burden of prayer during the meeting. There was a young wife, an ex-Volunteer officer, there, who had been backslidden for several years. God laid her heavily upon my heart and I felt she must be saved that night. The meeting was about to close, but she still sat unmoved. It was after eleven o'clock. I spoke to her and warned her it might be her last chance. Still she sat indifferent. Then I began to plead with her. The people resented this as I pressed her for a decision. They thought I was going too far. But an agony of prayer was upon me for her soul. I had to resist the opposition of the most of the other workers, as well as the enemy. For a full hour I battled thus, almost alone. At times I was driven back by the unequal conflict, and even tempted to think I must have been mistaken as to the mind of God. Finally I fell to the floor under a real travail of soul for her. It was the crisis. My life seemed almost pressed out of me. I felt a little bit of what Jesus must have felt in Gethsemane for us. This kind of prayer costs. Then all at once the burden left me. It fell on her. Conviction seized her. She fell to the floor as though shot and began to cry in an agony of soul. And so for nearly three hours she struggled and wept her way through, with a broken heart, to Calvary and to restoration. It was about 3 A. M. when she arose, with the very shine of an angel on her face, in perfect victory. It had paid to hold on to God and obey my convictions, be obedient to the Spirit. She confessed she had been very near the "dead line" that night, in her resistance to God. This sister later received a ministry of intercession, and was used of God in a marvelous way in soul travail in the meetings.

One night while preaching at Hermon a preacher jumped to his feet and cut my message off. He said he had to go home and wanted to testify. After speaking for some time he sat down. He had destroyed my message and the Spirit was greatly grieved. I did not resist him but committed the whole matter to God. The meeting was ruined. I did not attempt to speak further. He remained for at least half an hour after he was through speaking. This same man had opposed me in other meetings before. The devil had put him on my track to hinder my ministry. But this time he had gone too far. God smote him. Two days later he wrote me for forgiveness, promising not to oppose me any more. He also returned to Hermon and asked forgiveness publicly in the meeting.

I went to Pasadena again and spoke at the little Alley Mission. My message was one of warning. The sinners had been terribly trifling with God. While I was speaking the spirit of prayer fell upon two sisters (Mamie Craybill, and Jessie Hewett, the sister lately so wonderfully reclaimed). I closed the meeting and called the workers to prayer, but no one stayed but these two sisters. They could not leave. The others deserted us in the battle. I could not leave the sisters alone. They were under heavy burden of prayer on their knees. The Lord held them. Then a spirit of prayer seized me also. The sinners crowded in upon us as we prayed and wept there before the Lord. Our burden was for them. The gang of toughs became almost demoniacal in their resistance. It was an "hour of darkness." The mission itself was located down a dark alley, in the middle of the block. We had no street lights there, and no police protection. The Spirit warned me three times that my life was in danger. By this time the hoodlums seemed thirsting for my blood. They were led by a German, a very wicked atheist.

They now accused me of hypnotizing the two sisters. We were in the lion's den, with no possible, natural way out. This gang had heard the Gospel, sat in the meetings, and resisted the Spirit, until they were capable of most any act of cruelty. I had to be willing to face martyrdom, if need be, at their hands. This was the real test I was up against. I thought of the wife and children at home, in Los Angeles.. But God took all fear away from me in that moment. It was a wonderful experience. Finally one more bold than the rest seized me by the shoulder and commanded me to get up and quit praying. I offered no resistance but threw my hands up and called on God. The martyr spirit was upon me. The fire of God seemed to encircle and possess me. I felt no fear. The next moment, to my surprise my assailant lurched forward on his knees and began to beg me to pray for him. He had gone too far. God had struck him. Seriousness seized the rest of the mob for a moment. But they soon recovered.

Two of them seized one of the sisters. She threw up her arms and shouted victory. The power of God fell upon her. Fear fell upon the gang again and they left her. The other sister by this time was on her feet praising God. They stood the test like soldiers. I believe they would have died willingly for the Lord that night. It was midnight and we could do no more good there. We were in a nest of demons. I turned the lights out and had the sisters pass out ahead that I might know they were safe. They passed the mob safely. But the gang was outside waiting for me. The German atheist stood with a short club in his hand, ready for me. I shook hands with the first two toughs I met, evaded the leader, and passed through their midst without a scratch, by the mercy of God. They could not touch me. No doubt they expected me to show fear. But God kept me in peace, without a tremor. They could not even follow us. We soon reached the lighted street and were safe. It had been a rough experience, but the Angel of the Lord had protected us. And we had not failed Him. The sisters were real heroines. Wife told me when I reached home that she had been awakened from sleep (just at the time we were in the most danger), and prayed for my safety, though knowing nothing of the trouble. She felt I was in danger.

The gang had mocked our tears and prayers for them that night. But they had not mocked us, but Christ. I had never seen such daring before, and had a feeling they might have to pay for it. The very devil almost seemed to possess them. Some had Christian parents too, and knew better. Only a little while after this several of these same young men met a sudden, unnatural and horrible death. One had his head cut off by a train, while on a motorcycle. Another was burned to a cinder at the top of a telephone pole, by a live wire. He was a lineman. A third was burned to death with gasoline. He was passing a repair shop with his motorcycle, near this same mission, in the alley, when a man threw a burning rag with gasoline out of the shop. It had caught fire accidentally. It caught the young man full in the face and killed him.

CHAPTER 5

~

From California to Maine

The latter part of March, 1907, I received an invitation to come to Conneaut, Ohio, with a check enclosed for fifty dollars. They wanted "Pentecostal" meetings there. The leader wrote me they were hungry for "Pentecost." I felt it was a call from God to go east but could not help wondering if they really knew what they were inviting for themselves. The letter seemed full of enthusiasm, the thing John Wesley so strongly discouraged and deprecated. His definition of "fanaticism" was, "expecting the end without the means." I did not cash the check, fearing lest they might be disappointed when they got through with me. They had to learn that "Pentecost" meant the dying out to the self-life, carnal ambition, pride, etc., etc. It meant for them to enter into the "fellowship of His sufferings," not simply to have a popular, good time. This I felt they did not realize. A real Christian means a martyr, unavoidably, in one way or another. Few people are willing to pay the price to become a real Christian, to accept the ostracism, false accusation, and condemnation of others. But God has only one standard for His church, for all time. Present day profession is for the most part a mere sham. Only a small percentage of it is real.

A man once asked Luther to recommend to him a book both agreeable and useful. "Agreeable and useful!" replied Luther, "Such a question is beyond my ability. The better things are the less they please."

"Except a man forsake 'all'," said Jesus, "he cannot be my disciple." This may require some qualification, or explanation, as to positive action, but the principle remains the same for all. The church since her fall in the early centuries has had altogether a mistaken conception of her calling, and of salvation. All believers are called to a one hundred per cent consecration. God has no two standards of consecration for the foreign missionary, and the home Christian. We cannot find it in the Bible. One is called to consecrate their all as well as the other, as God's steward, in their own place and calling. One goes, one prays, and one gives. It takes the three to make a missionary. "This is a hard saying. Who can hear it?"

God has had but one purpose, and interest, in humanity since the "fall." That has been to bring man back to God. The whole old dispensation, with its providential dealings, was unto this one end. God had one recognized people, the Jews. He had one purpose in this nation. All their operations were to one end. All their worship pointed to that one end—to bring back the race, nations, to the true knowledge of God, and to bring in the Messiah of the world. Jesus Christ had but one interest in coming to this earth. His second coming waits for but this one thing also. When this Gospel shall have been preached in all the world "then shall the end come," the "curse" be lifted. Is the church working, with all her resources, for this one purpose, and to this one end? That certainly does not mean the selfish heaping up of property and riches, more than we really need. It does not mean getting all we want for ourselves, and then tossing the Lord a dollar we do not need. We have had the order totally reversed since the early church's fall. God requires exactly the same consecration of all. And here is where the Ananias and Sapphira business has come in. Not "one-tenth," in this dispensation, but "all." Our bodies are the temples of the Holy Ghost, and we are to be one hundred per cent for Him at all times. We belong to Him. He has created us, and bought us back, redeemed us, after we had mortgaged His property, not ours, to the devil. In no sense are we our own. We are redeemed back, with the "blood." How long would it take, or have taken, to evangelize the world under this rule? Think on these things! Is the church moving normally, in divine order? The politico-religious system, since the early church, and today, is largely a hybrid, mongrel institution. It is full of selfishness, disobedience, and corruption. Its kingdom has become "of this world," rather than a "heavenly citizenship," calling, with spiritual weapons.

The doctrinal issue has also been a great battle. Many were too dogmatic at "Azusa." Doctrine after all is but the skeleton of the structure. It is the frame-work of the "body." We need flesh on the bones, the Spirit within, to give life. What the people need is a living Christ, not dogmatic, doctrinal contention. Much harm was done the work in the beginning by unwise zeal. The cause suffered most from those within its own ranks, as always. But God had some real heroes he could depend upon. Most of these sprang from the deepest obscurity into sudden prominence and power, and then as quickly retired again, when their work was done. Some one has well said: "Men, like stars, appear on the horizon at the command of God." This is a true evidence of a real work of God. Men do not make their times, as some one has also truly said, but the times make the man. Until the time no man can produce a revival. The people must be prepared, and the instrument likewise.

The historian D'Aubigne has well said: "God draws from the deepest seclusion the weak instruments by which He purposes to accomplish great things; and then, when he has permitted them to glitter for a season with dazzling brilliancy on an illustrious stage, he dismisses them again to the deepest obscurity." Again he says: "God usually withdraws His servants from the field of battle only to bring them back stronger and better armed." And this was the case with Luther, shut up in the Wartburg, after his glittering triumph over the great ones of earth at Worms.

D'Aubigne writes again: "There is a moment in the history of the world, of such as Charles II, or of Napoleon, which decides their career and their renown. It is that in which their strength is suddenly revealed to them. An analogous moment exists in the life of God's heroes, but it is in a contrary direction. It is that in which they first recognize their helplessness and nothingness. From that hour they receive strength of God from on high. A great work of God is never accomplished by the natural strength of man. It is from among the dry bones, the darkness, and the dust of death, that God is pleased to select the instruments by means of which he designs to scatter over the earth His light, regeneration and life. Strong in frame, in character and in talents, Zwingle, whose defect consisted in this strength, was destined to see it prostrated, that he might become such an instrument as God loves. He needed the baptism of adversity, and infirmity, of weakness and pain. Luther had received it in that hour of anguish when his cell and the long galleries of the convent at Erfurth re-echoed with his piercing cries. Zwingle was appointed to receive it by being brought into contact with sickness and death."—D'Aubigne.

Men must come to know their own weakness before they can hope to know God's strength. The natural strength and ability of man is always the greatest hindrance to the work of God, and to God's working. That is why we had such a deep dying out, especially for the workers and preachers, in the early days of "Azusa" Mission. God was preparing His workers for their mission.

In answer to prayer the Lord opened the way for us, as a family, east. I carried my check from Conneaut, Ohio, in my pocket, uncashed. Wife wanted to see her people in New York State, and I did not know when I would be ready to return to California. I wanted to be free for God's full will. I remembered then, for the first time, that I had prophesied when we left Pittsburg for the west that we would be back in five years' time. God must have shown me, for it was now exactly five years.

Mother Wheaton, the prison evangelist, and Brother Amil Allen, traveled with us. We got a pass part way. At Salt Lake City we saw the Mormon Temple, held a service in the penitentiary, and then ran on to Denver. Ruth and John, our two children, were taken very sick, but God delivered. I preached at Holiness headquarters one night in Denver. Here we had been members and labored before we came to California. I preached for Brother Fink at the Pentecostal Hall, and we had a powerful time. Several souls were saved, among them one whole family, and the saints were wonderfully built up. Some received the "baptism." I had three meetings in all. God wonderfully used two little girls here. They both had the "baptism," and a real ministry of prayer. Their pleadings with the unsaved broke up the house. Their freedom from self-consciousness was a powerful lesson to us all. It was a strange work and ministry of God. Terrible conviction was upon the unsaved. "Except ye become as a little child," we learned anew. Evidently modern evangelistic methods are not altogether essential for the salvation of souls. The churches can possibly beat us on that line. We had better stick to our peculiar gift, though it be a "strange work." We will succeed better at that. Let God have his way. In those days the power and presence of God among us often converted sinners in their seats. We did not have to drag them to the altar and fight with them to get them saved. They did not come to the altar to fight God. There was much of the "singing in the Spirit" at Denver, as at "Azusa." This peculiar "gift" seemed to accompany the work wherever it broke out.

At Chicago we stopped at Beulah Rescue Home. I preached in the Home, and also at Brother Durham's mission, on North avenue, under a most precious anointing. I preached three times also at S. B. Shaw's mission, the author of the little book, "The Great Revival in Wales." We finally reached Conneaut, Ohio, April 30, in a snowstorm. God had shown me in Los Angeles that I would start my meetings there May 1. They tried to hurry us through a month sooner. But we kept in divine order. The presence of the Lord was with us in Conneaut, from the start. It was a Holiness mission. We really had little to do in the main but look on and see God work. The Spirit took the meetings. In fact we were on our faces most of the time in prayer. I could hardly keep off my face at Conneaut. The battle was the Lord's. And no one else could have fought it there. We were up against most stubborn resistance. The Lord had warned me of this condition before we left Los Angeles. The leader who had written inviting me had not the slightest idea what "Pentecost" meant, just as I had feared. He wanted a big time, with a big increase in the mission, to build up the work in numbers, etc.

I soon found him planted squarely in the way. While professing holiness he was tremendously alive to his own importance. God exalts no man or mission, but rather humbles all in the dust together, that He alone may be glorified. "The heart is deceitful above all things, and desperately wicked." Only God knows it. Sister Ivy Campbell, from "Azusa," was there with us. God had sent her on ahead some time before, to blaze the way for us. Her home was in Ohio. Brother Kennedy, a Wesleyan Methodist preacher, had been preaching for them. He was a most humble man of God.

The Lord wrought very deeply. Several were under the power all night on one occasion. There was no closing at 9 o'clock sharp, as the preachers must do today in order to keep the people. We wanted God in those days. We did not have a thousand other things we wanted before Him. And He did not disappoint us. One sister sang and spoke in "tongues" for five full hours. Souls were saved. The saints were wonderfully built up and strengthened by the presence of the Lord. A number received the "baptism," and the mission became full fledged for "Pentecost." One Sunday night the hall was packed out, to the middle of the street, I went to the hall one morning to look up the folks, who had not come home. Several had stayed all night. I found them lost to all but God. They could not get away. A very shekinah glory filled the place. It was awesome, but glorious.

Our big fight proved to be with the leader, who had sent for me. The meetings had not gone far until we found him wedged squarely in the way. One sister nearly died under a travail of soul for him. He was fleshly, proud and self-important, and would not let the meetings go deeper. We could go no further. He did not seem to have the least idea of humbling himself with the rest of us But he had to come down. God showed me I must deal with him. I had to obey, or quit. There was no use going any further. We were eating at his table and sleeping in his beds. It was a hard thing to have to do. But I went after him. We locked horns and he resisted me fiercely. But God brought him down. The Spirit convicted him and he fell in a heap. He almost jarred the building when he fell. He lay under a bench for five hours and began to see himself as God saw him. The Spirit took him all to pieces and showed him his pride, ambition, etc. Finally he got up, without a word, and went home. There he locked himself in his room and remained until God met him. He came out from that interview meek as a little lamb, and confessed his shortcomings. The hindrance was out of the way and the meetings swept on in power. He got the "baptism" himself some time later, after we had gone.

Brother Kennedy bought me a new suit of clothes before I left. So the Lord rewarded me for my faithfulness, and He did not have to depend on the leader, either. It pays to obey God. I visited Brother Thomas K. Doty, editor of "Christian Harvester," at Cleveland. Here I also preached with much anointing, for Brother Kramer, at the C. M. A. I spoke for two solid hours. I cashed my check here, that they had sent me from Conneaut to come east on. The meetings had been a success and all were satisfied. They gave me an offering, besides.

Our next meeting was at Youngstown, Ohio. Here I preached for the Christian Missionary Alliance. Some nights we were held in the hall until daylight. We could not get away. God was so near no one felt tired or sleepy. I had much real soul-travail here. In some meetings suppressed groans were about all one could hear. Very much prayer characterized the services. The Spirit was waited upon for every move, and He took complete control. No two services were alike. In one meeting the very silence of Heaven took possession of us for about four hours. Scarcely a sound was uttered. The place became so steeped in prayer and sacred that we closed the door softly, and walked the same, scarcely speaking to one another, and then only in whispers. Another night we were held in adoration and praise for hours. We seemed to be looking into the very face of God. There was no boisterousness in these meetings, but a subdued spirit throughout.

Another night we were all broken up by the love of God. We could do nothing but weep for a whole hour. Every meeting was different, and each seemed to go deeper. Two or three whole nights were spent in prayer. One night the Spirit fell upon us like an electric shower. Several went over on the floor and God was master for the time. Such singing in the Spirit, the "heavenly chorus," I have seldom heard. A number came through speaking in "tongues." But again our battle was with the leader. He opposed me fiercely. He was not right with God, and would not yield. His wife was now under the power, seeking the "baptism," but he carried on in the "flesh" until the Spirit was terribly grieved. The devil often gets into a preacher's coat. Satan used him persistently in the beginning of the meetings. But God got the victory, in spite of him. He did not yield. It is amazing the hold the devil has on some preachers.

I preached one night at Akron, Ohio, for Brother McKinney, with much blessing. We then had five services at New Castle, Pennsylvania, with the C. M. A. again. God greatly blessed here also. From here we went to Alliance, Ohio, for the Pentecostal camp meeting. It was June 13. We had a wonderful camp. It was the first one of its kind in the northeast. I led the preachers' meetings. The first Sunday morning I was given a message, but the leader asked me to speak in the afternoon, instead. I said nothing, but prayed. In a few minutes he came back and told me to preach in the morning. In those days men did not get far without God. I preached with great help from the Lord on, "Jesus Christ, in World-wide Evangelism, in the Power of the Holy Ghost." Everything centers around Jesus. We may not put the power, gifts, the Holy Ghost, or in fact anything ahead of Jesus. Any mission that exalts even the Holy Ghost above the Lord Jesus Christ is bound for the rocks of error and fanaticism.

This was a very important camp, in the inception of the work in that part of the country. We remained two weeks, and I preached eleven times in all. We had a powerful time and a large, representative attendance. Four hundred camped on the grounds. Often meetings lasted all night. Missionary enthusiasm ran high. Meals were on the free-will offering plan. God bountifully provided and a precious spirit of unity prevailed. We were "brethren," baptized in "one Spirit," into "on body." Thus Jesus' prayer was answered, "that they all may be one." The harmony between the preachers was especially blessed. Such a spirit of love we have seldom seen displayed. Those were wonderful days. It could be truly said that in honor we preferred one another in those days.

No organ or hymn books were used. The Spirit conducted the services and there seemed no place for them. Hundreds definitely met God. Numbers were saved, baptized in the Spirit, and healed. Many received a call to foreign fields, to prove God along real faith, Bible lines. The rapid evangelism of the world, on real apostolic lines, was the goal set. The present generation must be reached by the present generation of necessity, or lost. The altars were seldom empty of seekers day or night. Men who had been both in the Wales and India revivals declared this to be the deepest work of all. We determined to fight nothing but sin, and to fear nothing but God. I asked the Lord for a certain amount of money, which we needed to get on east. The committee gave me exactly the amount I had prayed for, without a single hint from me. God did it. Praise Him!

I took the wife and children to my father-in-law, near Peekskill, New York. He was a Methodist pastor, living six miles back in the hills, in a beautiful, hid-away, quiet place. Here they remained while I ran out to conventions, etc. I preached three times, the first Sunday, for my father-in-law, but both he and his churches were spiritually dead. Some of his official board both smoked and drank. I could do little for them. They did not want what I had. In New York City I visited Stephen Merritt, and attended a service at the C. M. A. headquarters. I also preached at a colored Pentecostal assembly. At Nyack (N. Y.) C. M. A. Convention, I spoke at two services, with much blessing. Some one paid my expenses there. I had not been invited. After a few days' rest with my family I went to Philadelphia visited the Grace Baptist Church, where I had once been a member, and from there ran on to Pittsburg. Here I preached for Brother Whitesides, at the C. M. A., afternoon and evening. I was to take the train the same night for Cincinnati, but could not stop my message in time. The people were so hungry. I preached for two hours. They gave me fifteen dollars, and I proceeded the following morning. This money paid my fare from Peekskill to Cincinnatti. The Lord was with me.

I stopped at Brother Knapp's Bible School, and next morning ran on to Wilmore, Kentucky, to attend a prayer convention. Here I preached seven times during the convention. The object of this camp was to develop unity among the brethren, and to raise up intercessors. S. B. Shaw and Thomas K. Doty were there. Rev. Shaw had invited me. But the camp was pretty well divided. Many of the saints were hungry for more of God. Conditions proved very detrimental to this. Brother Pickett had charge of the camp and charged a gate fee. This was mercenary. The holiness manifested I felt was of a rather acrid nature. It was not a "Pentecostal" camp.

I was taken quite sick with fever here but a missionary from India prayed for me and God broke the fever. Both the food and the water were bad. The convention voted me twenty dollars. This paid my fare home, to my family. I had traveled eighteen hundred miles. It seemed a long trip as I had never been more than a hundred miles from my family before. Our train ran over and killed a man on the way south. How uncertain is life! Brother Doty wrote in "Christian Harvester," concerning this camp: "There was loftier preaching, but Brothers Bartleman and Shaw were probably the greater prayer contingent for the work in hand." So I thanked God, and took further courage.

I next went to Old Orchard, Maine, changing cars at Boston. There was a C. M. A. Convention at Old Orchard. Some souls hungry for "Pentecost" arranged a meeting in the woods and invited me to speak to them. The Lord visited us in a most wonderful way. The devil had tried to keep me from coming here. The trip would cost me at least twenty dollars, and I was not invited. But I knew God had sent me. One evening I had been praying in the grove with a visiting preacher from Scotland. He suddenly took me by the arm and led me up onto the platform, seating me beside himself. He was to preach that evening. He wanted me to pray for him. It was a bold thing to do, but he was a fearless man. I knelt in prayer while he spoke and God greatly helped him. I had never met him before that evening and have even forgotten his name The leaders were greatly surprised to see me on the platform, but it was not my doing. I did not, however, venture on again.

A score of hungry souls repaired to the village church for a whole night of prayer, having secured the key from the local pastor. We were not allowed to tarry on the camp grounds. One member of the Nyack C. M. A. faculty got the "baptism" that night, and a backslider was reclaimed. I spoke to this little company in the church the next afternoon and evening, as they would allow no meetings of this kind in the camp. The camp meeting committee then forced the pastor to close the church against us. They did not want their people to get the "baptism." We went to the woods again. There I spoke the next morning and evening to a good sized congregation. I had nothing to do with arranging these meetings. There were so many hungry for "Pentecost" they insisted on my preaching to them. I did not dare deny them. I spoke in all about four hours that day. The committee had no jurisdiction over the woods outside the camp. I am sure Jesus would not have refused these hungry souls the bread of life. There was no less than one hundred people at the woods meeting. And all hungry for God. Surely He had sent me there for that purpose.

They pressed about thirty dollars in money into my hands. So the devil had lied to me. I came out ahead of all expenses. One sister, who had been a physician, ran after me one day and begged me to receive twelve dollars restitution money that was burning a hole in her conscience. She could not locate the party she had wronged, so turned it over to the Lord. That was a real work of God. The Lord had blessed so mightily in our little meetings that the camp became stirred. Rather than have further, outbroken trouble, the saints thought it best to discontinue the meetings, and I dropped quietly out of camp before the committee could take any definite further action in the matter. Thus we avoided further unpleasantness and strife. The hungry ones were fairly dogging my steps and thronging me. The committee became afraid of my influence with the people.

I stopped a few days at the Moody Convention, at East Northfield, Massachusetts, where I had attended years before, while a young student. Here I had a good rest and took some part in the meetings. Returning to my family, I removed them to my parents' home at Michener, Pennsylvania. I had not been home for several years. Here I spent a little time with them, resting, and studying the Word. They were very glad to see us. They had never seen the children. Near here I had been raised on a farm, as a boy. At Carversville, near by, I preached in the Presbyterian Church. My older brother, Will, heard me preach here for the first time.

It was now September. I went south to Columbia, South Carolina, preaching a number of times at the Oliver Gospel Mission there in connection with the "Way of Faith" office, where Brother J. M. Pike was editor. I had written many articles for this paper. We had much blessing in the services and I had a good visit with Brother Pike, whom I had never met before. I wrote two articles while here. A sister in New York City sent me ten dollars, Brother Pike gave me fifteen dollars, and another party gave me three dollars. So the Lord provided for my expenses again. I dropped off at Dunn, North Carolina, where Brother Cashwell's family lived, and preached five times in the little Pentecostal Church there. Brother Cashwell had gotten his "baptism" earlier, at "Azusa" mission, and had spread the fire in the south. He was away from home at this time. Brother Pike wrote in the "Way of Faith," after my visit: "Brother Bartleman dropped in upon us, unexpectedly, last week. His presence was a benediction to us and our home. His services were made a blessing to those whose hearts are longing for the Pentecostal blessings. None who have intercourse with him can doubt his absolute abandonment to God, and the fulness of the Spirit within him. He lives, moves and has his being in the will of God. We commend him to all who are seeking God's highest and best." —"Way of Faith." We hesitate to reproduce in print such a high commendation, knowing we are not worthy, but do so in order that we may have it before us continually as a goal to be striven to attain to.

The Lord was wonderfully with us in those early days. I preached six times in Washington, D. C., reaching my family again safely, at Michener, Pennsylvania. At Forty-second Street Mission, New York City ("Glad Tidings Hall"), we had powerful times. I had developed brain fag in the long and constant work in California, but this began to leave me now. What I needed was a change. That is the best rest after all. I visited Nyack, New York, again, preaching three times at the C. M. A. Then I removed my family to Philadelphia, to my brother Will's. Returning to New York City I attended the C. M. A. Convention at the Tabernacle. The saints paid my board, at the Alliance House. Just before I arrived there was not a vacant room in the house. But the Lord emptied one almost the moment I reached there and I was dropped right into it. Rooms were in great demand. A brother gave me ten dollars besides. The Lord had spoken to me upon arriving there: "Let there be no strife between us, for we be brethren."

I spoke for three hours one night at "Glad Tidings Hall," while here. Then the people wanted me to continue. They were so hungry for the "Pentecostal" message. I stopped at 11:40 P.M. Workers kept coming in from the Alliance convention, after the meeting closed there. But the devil fairly tore up the earth at the beginning of the meeting, through the rabble outside. He evidently sensed something of what was coming. The next night I preached again and many were prostrated under the power. Some stayed all night. The evangelist in charge of the night meetings at the convention came in himself, after the services had closed at the Tabernacle.

The next night they had an all-night meeting at the convention. A young girl came under the power and her spirit was caught up to the throne. She sang a melody, without words, that seemed to come from within the veil, it was so heavenly. It seemed to come from another world. I have never heard its equal before or since. A. B. Simpson was there himself that night and was tremendously impressed by it. He had been much opposed to the "Pentecostal" work. Doubtless God gave it as a witness for him. Several were slain under the power. Toward morning the presence of the Lord was wonderful. I went to leave the hall just at daybreak and shook hands with a sister hungry for the "baptism." The Spirit came upon her and I could not turn her loose until she fell at the altar, and came through speaking in "tongues." I shook hands with another hungry sister, as I started to leave the hall again. The Spirit fell upon her and she received the "baptism" right there on her feet, speaking in "tongues" before I could turn her loose. That was a wonderful night.

It was now time for us to start for California again. October 16, 1907, we left Philadelphia, stopping at Pittsburg, where I preached twice for Brother Whitesides, at the C. M. A. again. God met us in a powerful way. Several received the "baptism." The last one came through at 1 A. M. I preached twice at

Beaver Falls, Penn., at a C. M. A. convention, stopping off between trains, by special request. God greatly honored the Word. At Alliance, Ohio, I preached three times. The Lord was powerfully with us. We then proceeded to Chicago, where I preached at Beulah Home, and at Brother Durham's mission again. At St. Louis we stopped with Brother Seeley Kinne for some time. I preached here eighteen times in all, to as hungry, humble, and appreciative a company as I have ever met anywhere. God was wonderfully with us. I spoke twice at Mother Moise's Rescue Home, and four times at the C. M. A. hall, with much blessing, also.

At Topeka, Kansas, I preached five times for Brother Foster. One of the meetings here did not break up until daylight. God drew very near. At Denver I preached seven times. The Lord wrought again mightily among the people, but the leader was not true. He came very near causing the death of our little boy, John. He held back the collection the saints had given for me, to buy himself a pair of shoes with. The shoes he already had were better than mine. When I went to buy our tickets for Colorado Springs I found myself short, and had to return to the house and get the balance of the fare from his secretary. He had left town, with my money. We missed our train, and were thrown into Colorado Springs after night. No arrangements had been made for the family. They thought I was alone. We were taken hurriedly to a house without fire the first night. Little John contracted congestion and nearly died. It was freezing weather. And all this because of the sin of the leader in Denver. He had resisted the Spirit greatly in our meetings there. God made him send me my collection later. Some years later he confessed he had faked "Pentecost." I am afraid too many leaders have done the same.

At Colorado Spring I preached six times. The Spirit flowed like oil. I have seldom found such liberty anywhere. Oh, the possibilities, where purity and unity reign! Brother Brelsford was pastor here. He later went to Egypt as a missionary. Trinity, Colo., was our next stop. I preached ten times here, to a very hungry band of saints. They were much strengthened and blessed. But the high altitude was hard on us. Then the devil had tried to ditch our train just before we arrived there. We came on to Los Angeles from here, over the Santa Fe railroad. One night our wheels began to slide, down a steep grade in Arizona. I put on the brakes with prayer. The Lord brought us through. But I slept very little for two nights. We saw several wrecks along the way, and came near jumping the track ourselves twice before we reached California. The high altitude was also a great strain on my nerves. I was very tired from the summer's strenuous work. We were glad to be back in California again.

We had checked our trunks to Los Angeles, not knowing where we would find our next home. But before reaching Pasadena the Lord showed me we should get off there. We did not expect anyone to meet us, though I had written Brother Boehmer that we would get back on that train. When we reached Pasadena, with no place to go, we found Brother Boehmer at the depot waiting for us. He took us to a mission home on Mary street they had just opened in connection with the Alley Mission. So God had it all arranged for us, without our knowledge. We were weary pilgrims indeed, needing rest. We arrived December 5, 1907.

We were scarcely located when I went down with a terrible attack of the grippe. Ruth and John were both sick also. The devil had tried to hinder our return, and now seemed determined to kill us. I had shooting pains like needles for three days, in my shoulders and arms, until I was almost insane. The saints prayed and I was delivered. I found the work had fallen back considerably. The saints were badly split up. The Spirit was bound also. The outside opposition had become much more settled and determined. It was the same condition in Los Angeles.

The saints had suffered greatly under the tyranny of a leader who did not himself have the "baptism," at the Alley Mission. I now helped them to pray him out of the mission and the home, and they were delivered. He had imposed himself on the work. He was a regular "dog in the manger." A larger mission was opened up on Colorado street, and I had some ministry there also. I found the power had been dissipated much. There was much empty manifestation. A great deal of it was simply froth and foam. This burdened me greatly. The spirit of prayer had been largely lost. In consequence much flesh and fanaticism had crept in. Prayer burns out the proud flesh. It must be crucified, cauterized.

One day I had a strong impression that Brother Allen was in town. We had left him east. Sure enough that very evening he walked in on us. He had just gotten back. The Lord had shown me. We now moved to 194 Stevenson Avenue, next door to Brother Boehmer, into a little cottage. The ministry of intercession was heavy upon me. I preached a number of times at Hermon, Eighth and Maple, and at Azusa Street. One evening at Azusa Mission the spirit of prayer came upon me as a rushing, mighty wind. The power ran all through the building. I had been burdened for the deadness that had crept in there. The temporary leaders were frightened and did not know what to do. They telephoned for help. They had not been with us in the beginning. Brother Seymour was out of town.

I was upstairs in the hallway. Others joined me in prayer. We went down stairs and the fire broke out in the meeting. But the leaders in charge were not spiritual. Other rulers had arisen that "knew not Joseph." They did not understand it. God was trying to come back. They seemed afraid some one might steal the mission. The Spirit could not work. Besides they had organized now fast and hard, and I had not joined their organization. And so it is largely today. Sign on the dotted line or we cannot trust you. We affiliate only with those carrying our papers. "Pentecost" took that thing out of us. Why go back to it? All who belong to the different divisions in the Pentecostal work today have not the spirit of division. But God would hold us to the ideal of the "one body."

The Lord showed me my place of hiding. I determined to follow Him. That is the place of power. Fear nothing but God, and obey Him. I spoke many times at Eighth and Maple, and at Azusa, and also at the Alley Mission in Pasadena, exhorting them to more earnestness, and to walk in the Spirit. I had suffered much in prayer in the bringing forth of this work, and felt I had a right to admonish them. Our great battle from the beginning was with fleshly religious fanatics, purporting to be of the Spirit of God.

CHAPTER 6

A Second Ministry East

Brothers Boehmer and Allen received the "baptism" about this time. March 11, 1908, I received a letter from Brother Sawtelle, leader of the Christian Alliance work in Portland, Oregon, to come north and hold some meetings for them. God had shown me that we would be called out again. I recognized His call. We were to go north and east again. Brother Boehmer now decided to go with us in the work. I felt we had come back to the coast largely to get him out. I was exhorting the saints all winter to push out in the spring for God. About a dozen followed us, to different points, as we started out again. I began to feel the world-wide call heavily upon me, also. The Lord seemed to show me the oceans must yet be crossed for Him. And this we realized later on. Like Peter the Hermit I felt at times like stirring all Christendom with my cry for a revival.

March 25, we started north, for Portland, Oregon. We reached Stockton safely. It was hard to leave Los Angeles. I saw a hardening coming over the work and was much burdened for it. Oh, that we might know "the time of our visitation," and lay up corn, not dissipate our blessing. We were to need it all, to be established, as the past years have proven. We have had our "seven years of famine," as well as plenty. I spoke six times at Stockton, where I found the "flesh" pretty strong. But God gave the victory. It was the same old story. **They were expecting God to baptize their strength, instead of their weakness.** I suffered much here physically, from cold and neuralgia.

Little John was taken very sick. We next stopped at Carrie J. Montgomery's Home at Beulah, near Oakland, for a few days. While here I visited San Francisco and went over the stricken city. I had not been there since the earthquake. In spite of two years' labor almost night and day to repair the damage, the whole city still lay practically in ruins. A few towers had gone up, in the shape of modern buildings, but they were only an apology for a city. There was still so much rubbish they could scarcely clear space enough to rebuild. Many streets were even yet so twisted, sunken, and raised, that it was difficult to make one's way along them. It looked like a straggling country town, largely gone to ruin, instead of the proud city it once had been. Many cheap wooden buildings had gone up. But the proud mansions still lay as they had fallen, in total ruin.

Sin seemed more openly rampant, if possible, than ever, the people more reckless and abandoned. Dens of infamy were running full blast in the very midst of the ruins where thousands of lives had been lost. Space was cleared, buildings run up, and the dance with death moved on. The dives were the first to be restored. God was openly defied. In fact boasting against Him could be heard on every side. What fools sin makes of men. A skull and cross-bones, illuminated by an electric light, adorned the entrance to one of the most infamous dives. I felt I wanted to get away. The wrath of God seemed hanging over the place.

We took the boat from here to Portland and had a rough voyage. Most of us were sick. But God brought us through.

Stopping at Astoria we got steadied up a little. We reached Portland in the morning, and wife and the children went by train to Auburn, Wash., to visit some friends we had known earlier in Los Angeles. I preached in all about twenty-four times in Portland, at the C. M. A. Brother Boehmer was with me. God blessed preciously, but we did not break through fully. There was too much opposition and conservatism. Altogether however, much good was accomplished, and the saints especially were greatly benefited and blessed. Brother Sawtelle was very kind to me. Later he left the Alliance, to enter a profession. He became discouraged because he could not go on with God in the Alliance, and so quit the work entirely. It was a very pitiful case. He was a good man. They gave me sixty-three dollars, while in Portland.

I ran on to Auburn, Wash., and found wife and the children well. After two days I started meetings at Tacoma. Here I preached ten times, at the Christian Missionary Alliance. God wonderfully blessed, and several received the "baptism." We had a very sweet spirit at this place. Great love and unity prevailed. The Lord was pleased with this. They gave me twenty dollars. At Seattle I visited Brother Gourley's mission, preaching there once. Boehmer and I took a little side trip by boat to Victoria, B. C., on Vancouver Island. I spoke at Brother Burns' mission in Seattle also. Taking my family from Auburn we left Seattle for Spokane, over the Great Northern railroad.

God gave us a furnished home to ourselves to live in while in Spokane. We could not have been treated more kindly. Brother Herbert Bursell had called us there. We found a strong company of fine saints at this place. I preached thirty-five times in all and we had some very powerful meetings. We were there three weeks. The meetings began in a home, but they opened a mission before we left. At times I had much soul travail. Often God broke through until I could not preach. We had powerful altar services. The saints were hungry for teaching. I suffered much from neuralgia at Spokane. Brother Boehmer left us here, to visit his brother, and unite with us east again. Besides our living expenses they gave us one hundred dollars. We needed a lot of money to make our next connection, so we did not have any too much. The love of the saints in Spokane for us was very deep.

We passed through Deer Lodge, and Butte, Montana, and near the Yellowstone Park, via the Northern Pacific railroad, on the way to Minneapolis. At Minneapolis I spoke four times in the little mission, to a precious company of saints. I visited Minnehaha Falls while there also.

We ran on from here to Chicago. I visited Zion City, and then preached at Brother Durham's mission. Our next stop was at Grand Rapids, Michigan. Here I preached once, and we passed on to Toledo, Ohio, where I spoke twelve times, at the Pentecostal Mission. We had very precious meetings. God especially favored me with illumination in the Word. They gave us twenty-four dollars here.

Our next stop was at Alliance (Ohio) Camp Meeting, where we had been the year before. I preached nine times at the camp. It was a harder fought battle than the year before. There had been much fanaticism and lawlessness developed. The "flesh" tried to run the meetings. I spoke on "soul-travail" with great help from God. The Lord began to break through. Little John was taken with convulsions and the devil tried to kill him. The saints were not under the burden as they needed to be. They were there too much to have a good time and get blessed. I preached one afternoon under a very heavy anointing. Just as we sat down at the supper table and were about to eat, the Spirit suddenly fell upon us. We had a table with "all things common." The Lord seemed to desire to show His pleasure at this condition. The fire ran through the whole camp in a powerful way. The supper remained untasted for an hour. Many went down under the power. It was a deluge. I preached again that night. On two occasions during the camp nearly fifty were swept down under the power at one time. There were many missionaries there. In fact the missionary spirit ran high. The newspapers were more abusive and untrue than ever. But they thus did our advertising for us, free. Many received the "baptism," numbers were saved, and quite a few healed. The supreme thought was that of Jesus' soon coming, and the evangelization of the world in preparation for this.

I was getting very tired in body and mind. At Grand Rapids the devil had seemed to take possession of the very children where we were staying, for my benefit. They would tear around the house until midnight, without a cause, simply to wear me out. I was so tired I could hardly live. At Toledo the enemy would catch the thoughts out of my mind while I was preaching before I could express them. I was under especial illumination of the Spirit at this place, capturing new territory from the devil. One can always tell in preaching when they have gotten onto new territory, not before recovered. The enemy is always discovered, and generally makes a furious attack upon you.

We stopped at Pittsburg next, at the Christian Missionary Alliance, with Brother Whitesides. Here I preached four times, and wrote five articles for the "Way of Faith." I preached three times also at Braddock. The saints gave me forty dollars. We went on to Philadelphia and I left my family with my parents at Michener, Penn., not far from there. Brother Boehmer had rejoined us at Alliance, Ohio, and was now with me again. We went together to Rochester, N. Y., stopping at Elim Home. Here I preached four times. I had the message one night, but the leader refused to let me speak, because I had already preached over an hour in the afternoon. She was not used to letting God choose His own way. Human reason prevailed with her and she took the meeting in her own hands. The Lord dropped it right there. A crank got up and wore them all out with a long harangue. Then they allowed me to get up and deliver my message. A great burden came on Brother Boehmer and myself one night after going to bed. For over an hour we were tremendously pressed by the Spirit in prayer. We felt it was for some one. The next morning a preacher in the Home told of having received the "baptism" during the night. Then we understood. The burden had been for him.

We started for Toronto, Canada, visiting Niagara Falls on the way. At Toronto I spoke at Brother Sawder's mission one night, and at Brother Hebden's another. At both places God greatly blessed us. We then went to Brother Craig's mission at Camden street. Here I spoke fourteen times in all. I preached also at the C. M. A., for Pastor Salmon, and at Sister Builder's home. One night the Spirit held us all through the service in silence at Brother Craig's. The Lord would not let me say a word, though the Spirit was heavy upon me. I tried never to speak unless God gave me something to say. Pastor Craig could not understand this. He had not received his "baptism," and was very brainy. He was a good man, but seemed oblivious to the influences of the Spirit. It requires a copper wire to receive and carry a current of electricity.

The Spirit wrought very deeply in the meetings at Toronto. But the leader was very much tried with me because he did not understand the Spirit. He expected things done the old way, new wine in the old skins. The Lord had given me a premonition of conditions in Toronto before I reached there. Thus the Spirit often prepared me for my ministry. The Lord would give me the message for the place and prepare me to meet the particular conditions and need. He put the quiet spirit on me for Toronto. There was too much "flesh" there. The first two or three days He would not even allow me to look around town to note the differences between English and American customs, though they were many. He did not want my spirit taken up with earthly surroundings. It was a close ministry. Later I was allowed to look around a little. The "fleshly" ones largely dropped out at the first message. They could not live in such an atmosphere.

We next stopped at Potter Brook, Penn. I spoke three nights there, but it was haying time and hard to get the farmers out. We went on to Elkland, near by. Here we had a great battle. A child had a whining demon, and a dog seemed possessed with barking. This disturbed the meetings greatly. I spoke four times at the latter place and many received help and blessing. We rode twelve miles with a hired livery wagon to catch the early morning train on the main line, and reached Michener, where my family were staying, that evening.

We next went south, to Falcon (N. C.) Camp Meeting. Here I preached eight times. One night I was burdened all night in prayer. I could not sleep. The next day God came in the camp in great victory. The Spirit helped wonderfully. A multitude of people were there. We had some great altar services and many souls were wonderfully helped. Sinners were saved, and saints filled with the Holy Ghost. Some were healed. I had asked the Lord for forty dollars from the camp, but He told me to ask Him for fifty dollars. The trip was quite expensive. At the close of the camp Brother Culbreth handed me just fifty dollars. I had not even hinted about money. Someone else handed me six dollars. In Toronto God had shown me that Brother Sawders, whom they had invited to this camp, would not be there. I was not invited nor expected but God had shown me I was to go in his place. This, of course, I had kept to myself. Sure enough, Sawders did not get there. God knew. The devil had thrashed me up to the last minute about going to Falcon without an invitation. It was an expensive trip. I had promised the Lord if He would give me forty dollars at Falcon, I would leave five dollars for the work there. But he gave me fifty dollars instead, and six dollars extra, to pay my pledge with. The Lord will never go in debt to us.

Dr. Hood wrote in the "Way of Faith," from the Falcon camp, as follows: "The preaching was of high order. We were sorry of the inability of Rev. J. E. Sawders to be present, but we are sure the Holy Ghost guided in the matter, for he sent us 'a man of God' with a message most timely, and direct from the throne. We refer to Rev. Frank Bartleman, whom I believe to be perhaps the most humble and saintly person with whom I ever came in contact. He came to the pulpit from off his knees, charged with the power of God, and would hold the large audience in a very quiet way for hours as he delivered the message for 'this hour.' I believe he is truly one of God's men for this day." —Dr. D. A. Hood. I record the above with humility and shame, and only pray that I may become at least somewhat like the high order this dear brother has so graciously accredited to me.

I wrote myself at this time, in brief, concerning the situation at Falcon camp, as follows: "The Spirit impressed me while at Toronto that dear Brother Sawders would not be able to get to Falcon, and made known His desire for me to go. So

I went without further call, just in obedience to Him. We are getting our calls that way these days, and God is also seeking to release us from the responsibility of choosing the workers ourselves. Dear Brother Culbreth was kind and patient, both toward friend and foe, in a most marked degree. Evidently God knows his man. An able heart of love is a most capable thing. Dear Brother Floyd Taylor reminded me of the little brown bird to whom God has given no fine plumage, but has recompensed with a most beautiful song. Doubtless God keeps some samples in affliction, for His glory. Mephibosheth was also 'lame in both his feet,' but he 'ate at the king's table,' and dwelt in Jerusalem.' (Brother Taylor was a cripple.) God bless these humble southern brethren. They have been an inspiration and an example to me." —F. Bartleman, in "Way of Faith."

Brother Pike, editor of the "Way of Faith," wrote regarding the Falcon camp meeting: "Rev. J. H. King, one of the regularly appointed leaders, preached with unusual unction and power, and the voice in preaching and prayer of Rev. F. Bartleman was like that of one of the old prophets, with the Pentecostal enduement superadded. 'From his knees to the pulpit,' may be literally said of this Heaven-anointed messenger, and though his bodily presence is weak, it is soon apparent that he is a man sent of God, and he speaks with authority. We have rarely heard more unctious preaching than that of Brother King on Sunday night, and Brother Bartleman on Monday morning." —J. M. Pike. I sincerely appreciated the kind words of Brother Pike on this occasion. We generally get enough of the other kind to keep us humble, but I really feared the brethren had overestimated me. I only prayed I might not prove too great a disappointment to them. They had at least set a goal for me to strive for.

We came back to Washington, D. C., where I spoke four times with much blessing. We stopped in the home of Mother Perry. A precious sister was restored in these meetings. We stopped at Baltimore, where I also preached four times. Brother Boehmer seldom spoke in public. He had a wonderful ministry in prayer, and traveled with me for that purpose. His ministry was a hidden one. But I am satisfied it had much to do with the victory in our meetings. God may perhaps reward him even more than myself though I did practically all of the preaching.

I removed my family from Michener to Peekskill, N. Y., to my wife's people, and then went to New York City and spoke twice at Forty-second Street Mission, for Pastor Robert Brown. From there Boehmer and I went to Boston, to attend a Pentecostal convention. It was a fierce battle. The "flesh" was simply rampant. I gave a message in the morning against the "flesh." Both afternoon and night a message was given in the same tenor, by different parties, both ignorant of the nature of my message in the morning. And yet the leaders would not heed. They confessed to me some years later that they were wrong on this occasion. They took their own way and came into great grief and shame. God is not mocked. They refused to be corrected by the Spirit. We next stopped at Springfield, Mass. Here I spoke three times, at the Christian Missionary Alliance Church, at "Rock Rimmon."

We stopped in Sister Weaver's home. She was a very wealthy woman. Brother Cullen was the pastor. He had been a missionary in South America, and spoke Spanish fluently. The Alliance later sent him to Portland, Oregon, to fill the place of Brother Sawtelle, whom they had removed to Texas. Brother Cullen was later drowned at Portland. He was a good man and his end seemed very pitiful.

Boehmer and I returned to Peekskill for a few days' rest, and then went west to Grand Rapids, Mich., to attend a prayer convention. Riding all night through Canada we reached Grand Rapids safely. Here we stopped in the Pentecostal Home, with Sister Noble. I preached a number of times at the convention. But we had a great battle. They opposed the Pentecostal testimony and experience. God had sent me there to stand for this. I had such a soul travail one evening I rolled off the bed onto the floor, and under the bed. The battle was awful. I tried to run from it, and called up the railroad station to find out when the next train left town. But the line was busy. While waiting my eyes fell on a Scripture motto just over the phone. It read: "My times are in Thy hand." The Spirit smote me with conviction. I had not felt clear in leaving, but was under strong temptation. We stayed and fought the battle out. God gave us victory. But I received no offering from this meeting.

We next went to Indianapolis. Here Boehmer bought himself a watch. At the same time he bought one for me, for a present. I was needing one. Thus the Lord rewarded me for my faithful stand at Grand Rapids. I had a feeling we were due for a freshet of God's power at Indianapolis, after our desert experience at Grand Rapids, and remarked as much to Boehmer. And sure enough, it came. We found a convention on at Indianapolis. This we had not known of. We had not been invited. But the Lord had appointed it.

Brother Copley, and the Brelsford family, were there ahead of us. The Lord gave me a number of messages. We had a wonderful time. In fact I had not felt the power of God in such measure for a long time. There was tremendous opposition also, but God gave the victory. The work had been split into two factions. They came together in the meeting but were not reconciled. At one meeting the Spirit was so mightily on me in the message that the opposing faction held on to their seats and stiffened their backs to keep from yielding. I have seldom seen such resistance to the Spirit of God, and by Pentecostal saints, at that. It was simply awful. One night they had arranged for foot-washing. I gave the message that night and by the time I got through I think they had forgotten all about the foot-washing. They were too busy getting right with God, and with one another. Their souls needed washing more.

The Lord blessed me much at Indianapolis. I was so glad I had obeyed Him and gone there. I was there by His invitation purely. But I seldom if ever had felt such a wonderful flow of the Spirit before. The message seemed to be fairly drawn out of me in preaching. I felt almost drawn off the platform by the hungry desire of the people. I could not talk as rapidly as the thoughts came to me and almost fell over myself trying to speak fast enough. At one meeting when I was through the slain of the Lord lay all over the floor. I looked for the preachers behind me and they lay stretched out on the floor too. One of them had his feet tangled up in a chair, so I knew they had gone down under the power of God. I stepped over near the piano, among the people. My body began to rock under the power of God and I fell over onto the piano and lay there. It was a cyclonic manifestation of the power of God. We left the convention with great victory. I had not received a penny since leaving home and the devil was tempting me much over the matter. But the Lord kept assuring me He would make it up to me later on. I had to take His word for it, for I could not understand the situation. It was a new one to me. But I knew God had spoken.

We proceeded to Alliance, Ohio, where I spoke twice to the Bible Students. Our next stop was at Beaver Falls, Penn.

Here I preached five times in all, at the C. M. A. Brother Rossiter was in charge. I had stopped here, between trains, the year before. We had a most precious and profitable meeting. I was much pressed in my body, being attacked by a terrible neuralgia pain in my stomach. Much of the time while preaching I had to hold on to the desk in front of me, and every effort seemed to drive a knife thrust through me. When I attempted to pray the very demons seemed to attack me, with extra pains. God was trying to get the leaders here into the Pentecostal experience and all hell was moved to oppose it. They were very precious workers. Sister Rossiter was especially deep in the Lord. I seemed to be battling for them, and for my own life also.

Brother Rossiter was a very active man, and very nervous. He could not get quiet. While I was preaching and the Lord wanted to get hold of him he would be running around looking after the ventilation, etc. The ventilation was all right, but he could not rest. The habit had grown upon him until only God could deliver him from it. This he himself realized, and begged me to pray for him. His mind was always at work. Nothing hinders God more than this, especially when waiting on Him for the "baptism." The mind must cease from its own operations and activities before God can get possession of it. And this is just where the death comes. We must be "sealed in the forehead," so to speak. Our own activities must die. The Lord chased dear Brother Rossiter all around the church trying to get hold of him. But He could not catch him while we were there. Otherwise he was a most blessed man. But the Spirit could not get His way with him. At Findlay, Ohio, some time later, I had a convention, where the leader was so nervous the enemy had him on his knees on the platform striking matches and examining the straps on the pedals of the organ, while I was trying to preach. When a preacher is out of the Spirit the devil can get him to do the most fool things to hinder the success of a meeting. God was trying to deepen the work there and get the preacher quiet. But He could not. Perhaps the most distressing experience I ever had with a preacher in the "flesh" was at a convention just outside of New York City. A representative company of saints were there from many points. It was in the early Pentecostal days. This preacher was determined to preach, though I was burning up with the message. He wore the people out with a blackboard demonstration of mere statistics, long drawn out, while the saints groaned and waited for the message from the Lord. It was too late when he quit. Most of the people had to go early. I suffered for months over this defeat for the cause of Christ. Years later I met saints who had been at this meeting. They declared they were still waiting for that message that had been hindered. They felt they had missed a message of peculiar import for that occasion. I have seldom had such an anointing. We sometimes hear people say, "My message will keep." If God has given you a message for the people present, and for that hour, it cannot keep. When God gave a message to the prophets of old, or to the Apostles, it was to be delivered at a certain occasion, to a certain people. And just so today with a real messenger of the Lord, who is led by the Spirit of God in his ministry. The message, if not delivered on time, is lost.

It is hard for preachers to get the "baptism." They must die to so much self-ability, activity, etc. It puts self absolutely out of business. To become nothing is too hard for them. They may lose their position, support, reputation, etc. But God has always something better for us. We will have nothing left but God when the Spirit is through with us. But most of us cannot trust Him, so we go on our own way, follow our own calling.

To be a real servant of God, obey His orders implicitly, with no plans of our own, is a path few care to tread. It comes too high.

Sister Rossiter was wonderfully visited of the Lord at this time. He laid hold of her in a very deep way for a deeper possession of her than she had ever known. But she struggled hard. I think she was afraid she might have to die to the Alliance. She was a blessed woman, a wonderful instrument for God. But to follow Jesus only is a very narrow way. We were kept awake all one night by the Spirit. No one could sleep. The Spirit was like a wind blowing through the house. We all prayed all night in our beds. Boehmer and I were stopping with the Rossiters. God wanted that pair for something far greater than they had ever known. What became of them later I have never learned.

Boehmer and I returned to New York City. I visited my family at Peekskill, and then returned again to New York City. We called on Sister Weaver, with whom we had stopped at Springfield, at her request. She had a home in New York City also. All the previous day the words of the hymn had been ringing in my ears, "God is faithful, etc." The Spirit had said to me when we left Grand Rapids, "Ye have need of patience," when tempted over the money phase of the situation. The evening before we went to see Sister Weaver I seemed to feel the promise was near fulfillment. Sister Weaver knew nothing of my sacrifice on my trip west. I had received only a very few dollars on that trip. The workers ahead of us got all the money at Indianapolis. I had paid out of my own pocket forty dollars.

The morning we went to see Sister Weaver, Brother Boehmer had asked the Lord to give me fifty dollars. He had means of his own at this time and was bearing his own expenses. I was also impressed to ask the Lord to speak to Sister Weaver to give me that amount. We were about to start for Columbia, S. C., enroute for California again, and we had very little money on hand. While we were on our knees praying at Sister Weaver's, before leaving her, the Lord told her to give me just fifty dollars. No one had said a word to her about my needs. She handed me that amount. So the Lord had kept His promise and given me my fare back that I had expended on my last trip, west. But I had to be willing to make the sacrifice in faith, and wait until the end of the trip to receive it back.

At New York City I spoke three times at Forty-second Street mission, and then went to Nyack, New York, C. M. A. Training School. One of the faculty, whom I knew, and who was Pentecostal, asked me if I would speak there again this year, and then we both broke out in a holy laugh. The Spirit witnessed His pleasure. The opposition was great by this time at the school. He arranged the meeting by telephone, as we were some distance from Nyack. The faculty were caught off their guard. Five minutes later they would have canceled the engagement if God had allowed them to. They subjected me to an attempted severe censorship before I went to the platform, as to what I would preach. It tied me up a little, but the Lord gave victory. I was speaking to the students. And they were a hungry lot. I was allowed to speak again the next morning, after sleeping in the building. God touched their hearts in the end. I returned to New York City and spoke four times at "Glad Tidings Hall." The Lord greatly blessed us. Next I took my family Peekskill to my brother Will's, in Philadelphia, and ran up to Michener alone to bid my aged parents good-bye.

Boehmer and I then took the train for Providence, R. I., to attend a convention. Here I was the principal speaker, speaking eighteen times in all. We had a time of suffering. The leader hindered me much in the spirit, wanting everything run a certain way. But I had to obey God. I was not playing religion. I would rather farm for a profession. The people were very hungry, but the devil tried to hinder my messages. The Lord had faithfully warned me beforehand of this very situation.

I had a peculiar experience at this convention. God was wonderfully blessing my ministry. Preachers and leaders were coming in from many points. The message was largely new to them. The Lord so preciously used me that some got their eyes on the preacher. The Spirit could not stand for this naturally, so one afternoon, with a full house, come to hear the speaker from Los Angeles, the Lord told me to go and sit back of the piano, out of sight, to the end of the meeting. It was time for the people to have this lesson. In those days I would rather have gone to the woods and prayed many a time than to come before the people to preach. I was tired of the adulations of the people, preferring to get away from them, and alone with the Lord. Some of them were very much tried with me, for they had no message that after noon. But God knew his business.

I asked the Lord to give me fifteen dollars from this convention, and the leader without knowing a thing about this, handed me just fifteen dollars in a sealed envelope, before I left. It was a small, poor mission. I was not covetous for money. All I wanted was the privilege of working for God, and being used in blessing to the people. But I needed help to get my family back to California.

We started south for Columbia, S. C. Here I preached for Brother Pike at the Oliver Gospel Mission. The "Way of Faith" office was in this connection. I got a little chance to rest and pray here, with my family. I had been writing for the "Way of Faith" for a long time. We had practically meetings every night, however. Much intercession for this work was given me. Many of our meetings were taken up largely with waiting on God. And He met us in a wonderful way. Brother Pike was himself much blessed in these meetings. He was a very precious child of God. I spok also at a Presbyterian church. I helped publish my little book, "My Story of the Latter Rain" (now out of print), while here also. While we were here one of the workers in the mission had the mumps. Brother Boehmer and I were called to pray for him. The Lord had shown me sickness ahead before we started south. But I did not understand it then. Brother Pike handed me forty dollars when we left Columbia. That helped to clear the way for California. I had written for the "Way of Faith" for years without pay. In fact I have never written for any paper for pay. I could no more do so than preach for salary. We take what God gives us. I have written as many as 550 articles for the religious press, with not more than a half dozen failing to get in print, but have yet to write a single one for pay. My labor has been one of love. "Freely ye have received, freely give."

Brother Pike, editor of the "Way of Faith,'" wrote as follows regarding the meetings we held with him: "A remarkable meeting is now in progress at the Gospel Tabernacle, Columbia, S. C. It is remarkable for the prolonged vocal and silent prayer that is being offered, and for the unusual manifestation of the Divine presence that is being realized. Brother F. Bartleman is supposed to be the leader, but he will do no leading unless consciously prompted by the Holy Spirit. So the meetings are left perfectly free to the Holy Spirit's guidance. It is very certain that for depth of spirituality no such meetings have ever been held in the Tabernacle before."

Brother Pike wrote again, so complimentarily of my visit to Columbia, that I almost hesitate to reproduce it. He set a very high mark for me. He wrote as follows: "We have been enjoying the companionship and ministry of Brother Bartleman for the past two weeks, and have received a stimulus to our faith, and learned lessons which will be of great value to us in our experience and work in the future. The prayers that have been bottled up in Heaven, and the seed that has been sown in our midst, are sure to produce marked results in the future. Brother Bartleman's quiet ways, and his insistence upon quiet, prayerful waiting upon God, will find ready acceptance only among those who are accustomed to intimate fellowship with the Deity, and who know the blessedness of stillness. We are fully persuaded that God has some remarkable manifestation of His presence and power in store for this Institution if He is permitted to have His own way, and much of it will be due to the intercession and influence of this devoted brother, who leaves blessings wherever he goes.

"We do not know the secret history of how this man of God was brought into connection with the "Way of Faith," but that the whole arrangement was of God we have not the shadow of a doubt. He is a man after the editor's own heart, and we are sure that his connection with this paper was brought about by God, in the fulness of time. The pressure of the Divine presence is sometimes so great upon him that food has no attraction for him, and possibly he sometimes errs on the line of abstinence. Hence his appearance frequently indicates weakness, if not emaciation. God has committed to him, in large degree, the ministry of intercession; but he has also given him special messages for the present time to the saints in every part of the world. They are being delivered in various sections of the United States, and Canada, by the living voice, and through the paper they reach the saints in all nations. We commend him to the prayers of God's people everywhere, for, be very well assured, that he has come to the kingdom for such a time as this." —J. M. Pike.

I think perhaps no one knows better than myself how far short I fall at all times of being worthy of such high commendation, but I give it here to show the wonderful spirit that existed between brethren in those days. If we erred it was on the right side after all. I wrote regularly for some years for the "Way of Faith," my articles for a long time appearing almost weekly.

We stopped next at Atlanta, Ga., where we received a hearty welcome from Sister Sexton. The Lord blessed our ministry much there. Brother Boehmer left us at Columbia, for Altamont Bible School. He later took up pastoral work for himself in the south. We were glad we had helped to get him into the field definitely for God. (He is still active in the work at this writing.) We had some blessed meetings in Atlanta. Little Ruth developed the mumps there. She evidently had contracted them at Columbia. Here then was the sickness the Lord had shown me before we started south. Little John began to show symptoms of them also. Hell began to rage. I was preaching twice daily.

My main message here was the revelation of Jesus in the "baptism." It was the same message God had held me to at Eighth and Maple. The great danger was of the people worshipping the sign of "tongues," rather than the Lord, thus making a brazen serpent of it again (a "piece of brass.") It must be Jesus first of all. The Holy Ghost reveals Jesus. Both Ruth and John had the mumps now. The question was, would wife and myself escape them. But I went on in the work, trusting God.

I left my family here and took a little side trip to Birmingham, Ala. Here I began to suffer much in my body. The mumps evidently were working on me, though I refused to acknowledge it. At Birmingham I had a fierce battle. I met some most precious saints there, but there were some very strange spirits working in the meetings. Brother Pinson was in charge. He was a precious brother, but he had his hands full. The devil evidently wanted to ruin the work. We had a fair share of victory and blessing in spite of the enemy. I began to suffer intensely in my body. I was sick. The spiritual fight was one of the hardest ones I had ever been in. This caused me much suffering in my spirit. The weather was also very hot.

I found many professing a very high state of holiness here. But there was much of "self," and the spirit was very hard. When "holiness" loses its sweetness it is a fierce thing to come in contact with. This was largely the condition among the opposers of "Pentecost" in Birmingham. A backslidden spirit can become positively devilish, and that in the name of holiness even. I preached ten times in Birmingham.

Returning to Atlanta we started for Houston, Texas. The children had recovered from the mumps. We passed over the same track at night, this time in a Pullman sleeper (the only kind they had on this train), that I had walked the ties over, some years before, as a street evangelist to Mobile. I had some hours between trains at New Orleans, and visited the French quarters there. We reached Houston Dec. 24, just in time for Christmas. I began to develop the mumps on the train the night before. Wife was also beginning to have them. We went to Brother M. E. Layne's home, I got our trunks from the depot, and went to bed, just in time. I was to have attended a convention there.

God had opened a beautiful home to us there, with every care. We could not have been treated more kindly. I had one of the worst spells of sickness I had ever had. What I suffered was awful. I felt like dying. My jaws locked solid until I could not get a knife-blade between my teeth. But for the fortunate fact of having some front teeth out I could hardly have taken any nourishment. After a week of awful suffering however I began to recover. Wife did not have them quite so bad and was able to wait on me. The Lord protected the family we were stopping with from getting them. We prayed they might be spared, after the kindness they had shown us. They had several children. After three weeks I was able to get out, though very weak, and spoke a few times at the close of the convention. Here I met Brother E. N. Bell for the first time. We can never forget the kindness of Brother and Sister M. E. Layne to us at this time, in whose home we were staying.

I wrote for the "Way of Faith" while sick in Houston, the following observations on the life of a pioneer Pentecostal evangelist, as follows: "The Pentecostal preacher of today is obliged to spend most of his life in old drafty halls, with the poorest kind of ventilation. That means constant tearing down. The nervous strain brings on neuralgia and chronic congestion, through constant cold contracted, and overwork, for there are so few to do this strenuous kind of work today. This means a "living sacrifice," and the evangelist must find a place to rest, or go under shortly. We have said nothing about the separation from one's family, whose company others are able to enjoy. Then there are hundreds of other things the people know nothing about, such as dangers in traveling, constant change in beds, food, climate, etc. And we have said nothing of the spiritual conflict, the centering of spiritual opposing forces in each battle, and the constant, awful pressure of the forces of evil of the highest order. One is drawn upon for their utmost resources constantly. The worker is on the floor so much, on his knees in prayer in the meetings, that cold drafts in drafty halls sweep the body constantly. It is hard to keep off your knees in the present work. In fact you are driven to your knees and face in prayer constantly, and that for hours at a time. The remuneration generally is little if any more than expenses paid, and the evangelist is simply a channel in constant, strenuous use, soon to be worn out, and often then cast aside. His only refuge seems to be Heaven. But Jesus is coming soon. Then we shall need nothing more." —F. Bartleman. Old worn out Pentecostal horses are too often turned out by the roadside, to pick what grass they can find, with poor teeth, until they mercifully die. They are not as a rule turned into a fat pasture, after they are of no more service, to end in comfort and free from care the remainder of their days. Many are under the sod already, from overwork and neglect.

Our next stop was at San Antonio, Texas. Our money was all gone. Little John was taken very sick again. I felt on the train a warning that the devil was about to attack him, but tried to throw off the impression. He had not yet shown any symptoms of sickness. But that night he had convulsions. We spent a terrible night fighting for his life, on our knees, in prayer. The very demons seemed to attack us. He had both grippe and the malaria. We were stopping in the home of Brother and Sister Smate. He was finally delivered.

I preached in all about ten times here. My back pained me terribly, and I was still weak from the mumps and the hot weather. The grippe was attacking me also. I preached at a tent meeting where I met with much fanaticism. My message ran three false prophets out of town. The devil fairly howled. There were many soldiers encamped here and I preached a number of times to these boys in a little mission. I was looking to God for our fare to Los Angeles, and received several letters from a distance with money, after a fierce battle in prayer, and we were able to get on to Phoenix, Arizona. The devil had seemed determined to kill us in Texas. While at San Antonio I visited the old Alamo fort and mission, where Davy Crockett had made his last, heroic stand.

We had a pleasant journey to Phoenix. Running along the Rio Grande we could see old Mexico on the opposite side. We passed through El Paso, and received a warm greeting at Phoenix. We were very tired, and did not have our fares from there to Los Angeles. They were very kind to us in Phoenix. A sister went to look for rooms for us, while I prayed. I soon had the witness that she had found what we needed. Sure enough, she returned soon, having secured housekeeping rooms for us. We now began meetings in a little mission conducted by Brother Scull. We were there nearly three weeks. I spoke twice daily, and three times on Sundays. We spent more time at the altar than we did in preaching, however. The Lord met us in a very deep way.

We had a hard fight with the devil to begin with. Someone threw a rock through the window one night. It just passed over our heads. We were praying with a poor drunk at the altar. The devil did not want to lose his servant. In fact he even sent a preacher all the way from Pasadena, Calif., to oppose me here. So the enemy met me before I reached the state line, to oppose my return to California. But God gave the victory.

Little John was taken very sick again at Phoenix. I battled for his life one whole night in prayer. Was much worn out myself by this time. The money was given us here for our fares to Pasadena, where the Lord showed me we were to locate in California. We arrived there safely February 26, 1909. We had prayed for a home, not knowing where to go. I sent a note to one of the saints that we were coming. Mother Wheaton and Brother Crary met us at the depot. A new Pentecostal Home had just been opened up, at 786 Winona avenue, and they dropped us in there. Thus God had provided again, without our foreknowledge.

I stayed at home over two Sundays, to rest up, and then plunged into the work again. I visited old Azusa Mission, where the Lord met me in great power. At Eighth and Maple He also blessed me wonderfully. I also visited the Upper Room Mission, at 327½ South Spring street. When nearly home one night, in Pasadena, on Winona avenue, about 11:30, two dogs came tearing out at me from a nearby yard. They were known as vicious and dangerous, having already bitten a number of people. Their owner had gone to bed. Strangely enough, just at the same moment the street light went out. It was "the hour of darkness." Hell seemed suddenly turned loose upon me. The attack was so sudden and unexpected I did not even have time to think. But I cried out instinctively the name of Jesus for help. Instantly the dogs fled from me as though they had been shot. The light came on in the street again at the same moment. It was a strange coincidence. I am sure the devil set the dogs on me. He evidently had the light turned off some way also. But God delivered.

The Lord met and blessed me wonderfully both in Los Angeles, and at Hermon, in preaching, after this. He often broke me up with His love until I would weep like a child, especially at the Upper Room Mission. The leader here opposed me much. His spirit was largely unbroken and he thought me weak. He even implied at one time that I was mentally unbalanced. But he did not understand the love of God. Charles G. Finney, the great evangelist, once said: "If you have much of the Spirit of God, it is not unlikely you will be thought deranged by many. You must make up your mind to be so judged, and so much the more as you live the more above the world, and walk with God."

CHAPTER 7

Visit to Hawaii.
Volcano Kilauea

I came home one night and found a letter waiting for me from Honolulu. For some time I had felt drawn to the Islands. Every day I would look at the foothills back of the Home in Pasadena, and something would say to me, "Hawaiian Islands." I had seen pictures of Hawaii that resembled these foothills. The letter was a complete surprise to me, coming from a party I had never known. When I saw it I felt at once before opening it that it was a call to come there. It contained a check for $165. I had never received so much money at one time in my life. Sure enough it was an urgent call to Honolulu, from Sister Henrietta Nuzum, and the saints there. In the natural I shrank from leaving my little family, to go so far, and across the water. But it was the voice of God. I dared not disobey.

I visited Azusa Mission and Eighth and Maple to say farewell. At the Upper Room Mission they tried to discourage me from going. Some even warned me of disaster if I persisted in going. But I knew the voice of God. The leader tried to discourage me from going. I had learned however, by bitter experience, long before this, even in the Holiness movement, that one must get their directions from God, and not from the mission leader.

I think one would seldom attempt anything for God if they were to listen to those who always seem ready to discourage you. No one can get our leading for us. We must hear from God ourselves. Very often we are discouraged by jealous parties who desire themselves such a call from God, but have it not.

I took my family north, leaving them at Sister Carrie J. Montgomery's Home near Oakland. They were to have reduced rates for board, and await my return from the Islands there. I felt led to labor in that section when I should return. I paid one month's board for them, and sailed May 15, 1909, for Honolulu. We had an exceptionally smooth voyage. I was sick the first two days, but not after that. The Lord met me wonderfully on the vessel just before I landed. He welcomed me Himself to the Islands. I was met again wonderfully by the Spirit when I reached the home of Brother and Sister Harold Hansen, in Honolulu, where I was to stay.

The "fragments" of the continents (the Islands), must be gathered up also, that "nothing be lost." I found the Hawaiian Islands a natural paradise. Tropical fruits and foliage greeted me. There were Hawaiians and Koreans, Chinese and Japanese, but a very small white population. The sea voyage was a great benefit to me physically. Six days travel away from the little family, and without seeing land, seemed a long way, however. I had never been so far from them before. It was 2100 miles from San Francisco. From here the "southern cross" was plainly visible in the heavens.

The power of God was wonderfully poured out in our meetings. They had no hall but we met in the homes of the saints. Many were greatly benefited and quickened in their faith. I took a trip to the largest Island, Hawaii, by boat, on the leeward side. We passed by the islands of Molokai, Mauie, Lanai and Kahoolawe. I stopped at Kailua, Kone, with a missionary who owned a home there. Dr. Yoakum had visited here before me. We were in the same latitude as Central America. A party of us rode horseback to the top of Mt. Hulalai, 9000 feet high, through very wild vegetation, up the mountain side, guided by a Portuguese cowboy. We had a wonderful trip and a magnificent view, visiting a number of extinct volcano craters. I sent another month's board home to the family from Honolulu.

After returning to Honolulu, I took another trip to Hawaii, this time on the windward side, to Hilo. I found this a very wicked place. While here I visited the active volcano, Kilauea. This was truly a very picture of the "lake of fire," hell proper. I wrote an article on the volcano, from which I give the following extracts: "We reached the 'Volcano House,' Kilauea, Hawaii, at dark, and started for the crater afoot, three miles farther on, in the center of a deep basin, over a floor of lava rock seven miles in diameter. It was cold and raining. Down several hundred feet, over loose sand, and then over the hard lava flows, jagged, rough and craggy, we plodded. The lurid light of the crater glared in the distance, like a great chimney, flaring and smoking against the murky sky. The surroundings were most uncanny. The trail was dim. We were on our way to the 'pit.'

"'Surely Thou settest them in slippery places.' 'Give glory to God, before He cause darkness, and before your feet stumble upon the dark mountain.' We crossed fearful chasms, rent by convulsions of internal conflict, from the fires of torment in earth's bosom. Hot blasts fanned us from beneath. Vapors of sulphur greeted us from the fissures. The whole earth seemed 'turned up as it were by fire.' Finally we reached the volcano. It was a terrible sight. 'Outer darkness' encompassed the lurid fires. Hot air greeted us fiercely, as we approached the brink. Sulphur fumes rose almost stifling from its depths. A very 'belly of hell.' Nothing was lacking but the forms of demons, and they seemed hovering near. The natives worship this crater.

"'Where their worm dieth not, and the fire is not quenched.' Truly 'salted with fire.' Here was a fire no one could explain. The splashing of its fusions struck the heart with terror. Like the just punishment for sin. They lashed themselves against the sides of that cavernous pit as if conscious of being confined only for a season. They seemed like living, 'eternal fires,' awaiting restlessly their prey. The 'pit' proper is 1000 feet in diameter. In it is situated the lake of fire. The dismal shadows, the lurid light cast upward on its deep, cavernous sides, by the continuous unrest of its fierce, fiery commotions, as though demons struggled with one another in fearful conflict, with the fumes of stifling sulphur that arose from its awful, abysmal depths in clouds to the top of the sheer, jagged precipices that mark the naked heights of its lonely confines, made it a picture terrible to behold. One stood solemn and awe stricken, as in the presence of offended Deity. The dark background of the mountain shadows, the rain and piercing cold of the night, all added terror to the picture. It made one, like Moses at Sinai, 'exceedingly fear and quake.'

"These fires, in mighty conflict of convulsion, threw up those mountain peaks, from three miles under sea level, to their present height of 13,000 feet above the sea. The 'pit' itself is 4000 feet above sea level. What an awful mass of uncontrollable, fiery matter must heave and roll beneath this monster chimney of the Pacific, in earth's belly. Are not God's fires eternal? I thought of 'the waves of the sea that cannot rest,' to which the wicked are likened. There is no rest in hell. 'The lake of fire that burneth with brimstone.' 'And the smoke of their torment goeth up forever and ever.' 'They have no rest day or night.' All the elements were there. It was a perfect picture.

Two great channels or fountain furnaces were pouring from their subterranean depths tons of liquid fire, molten world matter, continuously. Billions of tons were heaving in seeming production. World making seemed in process. One seemed to be standing by the Almighty as at creation's dawn, when worlds were flung into far space, spoken into being by His fiat. But what makes these fires? What keeps them going? There is no answer from their abysmal depths. They scorn to answer. It is God.

"Their noise, between a hiss and a roar, like the cry of a wounded serpent or beast, seems crying for vengeance. They dashed against the sides of their unwilling confines, by force of continuous, internal conflict, with a cry almost human; then lashed themselves into greater fury, in their disappointed effort for liberation. What could man do once these fires were liberated?

"There was no rest for the fiery waves in that volcano. They rose by their mighty fusions, some forty feet high, all over this lake of fire, continuously night and day, only to fall back again baffled, with a sickening, terrifying thud, like the muffled rumbling of distant thunder. Their failure to scale their prison walls seemed but to enrage them more. As they lashed themselves against the sides their matter cooled, clinging to the rocks of their own production, but to encase and entomb them further. Others fell back, only to be fused again in that awful furnace of unbearable heat and fury. There is no escape from hell. A million years but makes the doom more sure in those lonely confines of despair.

This mighty stream of molten lava was churned continuously into an underground passage at the other side of the lake. And still those two great feeding furnaces poured their red hot, molten matter from God knows where, to where God only knows, by some subtle, awful power, in a continuous, fiery flow. There is no Niagara to quench its fires. Its torment is only increased by its continuous, constant action. There is a fire that feeds itself, a worm that 'never dies.' 'It is a fearful thing to fall into the hands of the living God.'

"There could be no trifling with the fires of that crater. The natives call it Pele. They say Pele was a woman. She was robbed of her husband by another native woman, who enticed him. Pele wandered from island to island (leaving extinct volcanos behind her), and finally settled on Hawaii in her wrath. The natives fear her. They throw bottles of gin, their favorite drink, to her, in order to appease her. And should not sinners fear a 'jealous' God? Presumption means swift, certain ruin. I turned from these lurid, mysterious fires in earth's bosom, with the weird surroundings of gloom that hung like a pall over the surrounding situation, with a feeling of awe, almost akin to terror. I shall not trifle with God." —F. Bartleman.

We had a rough voyage home from Honolulu. I brought a large basket of tropical fruits with me, for the family. The Lord had kept them safely in my absence. I preached at Beulah Chapel, at Sister Montgomery's a few times, then took a trip to Ukiah, Santa Rosa, and Healdsburg, holding several meetings. God was with me in power. I then preached five times in Oakland, at Barney Moore's tent. My next trip was to Woodland. Here I delivered my message under great affliction and suffering. The saints were in a peculiar condition of need. The evening I reached there I was seized with a terrible attack of appendicitis. It looked like death. The pain was terrible. I cried to the Lord in desperation and He delivered me. But a bad state of stomach neuralgia and colic remained. I could scarcely eat and got no sleep at nights. I could neither sit, lie down, nor walk without most severe pain. But in spite of this I delivered my message, remaining several days. My visit delivered the work from much extravagance that had killed the Spirit, but it nearly killed me also.

I had a blessed ministry at Stockton, preached a number of times more at Beulah and at Oakland, and then took my family to Santa Cruz. Here they visited with friends while I went to San Jose, preaching six times at the Pentecostal Mission there. The Lord greatly helped me. The saints were badly split up. I spent three whole days in prayer in the mission. My message was a plea for love and unity.

We then returned to Los Angeles, and located at 163 South Gless street. We had learned through a brother that Sister Throop had rooms about to be vacated. I phoned her from the depot and learned the rooms had just been emptied, and were for rent. The Lord had timed our arrival exactly. God had shown us to come, but we did not know where we should locate.

The missions, I found, were very zealous for doctrine, as usual. I began to preach at Eighth and Maple, Azusa Mission, and Hermon. Azusa had lost out greatly since we left. "How are the mighty fallen," came to me most forcibly. But the Spirit came upon three of us mightily in prayer one evening there. He assured us He was going to bring the power back to Azusa Mission again as at the beginning. We felt we had prayed through. (And the answer came a little over a year later, when Brother Durham came from Chicago. The place was then once more filled with the saints, and with the glory of God, for a short time.)

The work had gotten into a bad condition generally at the time we returned to Los Angeles. The missions had fought each other almost to a standstill. Little love remained. There was considerable rejoicing, but in the "flesh:' A cold, hard hearted zeal, and human enthusiasm, had taken the place of divine love and tenderness of the Spirit largely. I suffered much from contact with this thing. The Lord continued to bless my ministry at Eighth and Maple, and at Azusa street. In some of the missions I met with persistent opposition, especially from the leaders. But I kept my eyes on the Lord. He has never allowed me to become the satellite of any man, even for a place to preach. If we are servants of men we cannot please God.

October 14, 1909, wife presented me with another daughter, Lois. God graciously undertook for her. My ministry was principally divided now between Eighth and Maple, Azusa Mission, and Brother Hill's. The Lord blessed much and I also started weekly Bible studies at Eighth and Maple. In this the Lord blessed richly. We had some times of real testing, being completely out of money at times, but God always came in time to save us from actual suffering.

At one time our gas bill and rent were both due. I went to Pasadena, out of money. A brother was debating in his mind whether to help me or not. But I walked away from him. The devil was tempting me and I determined to trust God and not man. I went home without a cent. Before bed-time another brother brought eight dollars to the house. It was the exact rent. He said the Lord told him to bring it and he dared not disobey. He was a poor day laborer, too. But he got his reward from God. He was able to give him ten times as much, with ease.

Nearly every night found me either at Eighth and Maple or Azusa street, preaching or testifying. We passed through another hard test for rent and food, but the Lord delivered. I received money from the saints in Honolulu on two different occasions, at one time ten dollars, and at another time fifteen dollars. The last time little John had volunteered to pray for money. We were about out of food. He went to his knees and put us to shame with his childish simplicity and faith in prayer. We had been sorely tempted. He asked us if Jesus would send us money if we asked Him. What could we say? Of course he would. Very soon the money came, from Honolulu. The Lord had answered before we called on Him, as He has said. "Before they call, I will answer." This strengthened John's faith greatly. "He knoweth of what things we have need before we ask Him." If this were not true He frequently could not get the answer to us in time.

Old Azusa Mission became more and more in bondage. The meetings now had to run just in appointed order. The Spirit tried to work through some poor, illiterate Mexicans, who had been saved and "baptized" in the Spirit. But the leader deliberately refused to let them testify, and crushed them ruthlessly. It was like murdering the Spirit of God. Only God knows what this meant to those poor Mexicans. Personally I would rather die than to have assumed such a spirit of dictatorship. Every meeting was now programmed from start to finish. Disaster was bound to follow, and it did so.

Many a God-sent "prophet" has been done to death, both physically and spiritually, in Los Angeles. God has been obliged to remove leader after leader for this sin. I had prayed five years for a typewriter. A sister gave me twenty dollars, and I bought a second-hand one for $12.50. This I carried around the world with me later, to write my diary with.

I now began to feel the Lord was calling me to girdle the globe on a missionary trip for Him. It was to be by faith, and

I had not a cent in sight. I had really felt the call to make this trip for years, and the time had now come. It looked like madness to attempt such a thing in the natural. I was just at that time up against a very severe test both physically and financially. But the conviction became an assurance. After a very severe financial test, in which it seemed almost impossible to get even as much as a ten-cent piece, the Lord opened the way for me to start. I believe God allowed me to be thus tested in order to prove me for the journey. It looked almost like actual starvation just before the way finally opened up.

Dr. Sister Trout gave me fifty dollars to put in the bank for wife to draw on for the rent. Then Brother Pike, editor of the "Way of Faith," sent me twenty-five dollars from Columbia, S. C. This was to used to start around the world, and with this amount I started. All this was absolutely unsolicited. I would not have dared to take a step in such a tremendous undertaking, impossible in the natural, had not God made it so plain to me that I could not doubt His will in the matter. Besides, to leave my little family without means, to go around the world, with all its possibilities for evil and disaster, to be gone nearly a year, would have been too much for a heart of flesh to bear, except God should guide fully and strengthen.

They gave me a little offering at Azusa Mission of eleven dollars. This I left with my family. I received no help from any other mission. It was all I had to leave them.

When I started to circle the globe I was warned by many of the saints not to attempt it. Some told me God had revealed to them awful disaster to follow, both for myself and family, should persist in my purpose. But I knew God had called me. I had to obey Him, and in doing so I realized one of the greatest privileges and blessings of my whole ministry. I felt I could read considerable jealousy between the lines in some of the letters I received. One sister even declared she did not believe the Lord was sending me because she had always wanted herself to go on such a trip and the Lord had not allowed her. Her warning naturally did not have much weight with me. I did not carry a single dollar with me from Los Angeles.

I left home March 17, 1910. (My world-trip is published in a separate book, to which the reader is referred, "Around the World by Faith, With Six Weeks in the Holy Land." —price 50¢.) Circling the entire globe by faith, visiting Europe and most of the principal mission fields in my course, I spent six delightful weeks in Palestine, returning home by way of Egypt, India, Ceylon, China and Japan, and across the Pacific, via Honolulu. I was gone eleven months and one week. My family trusted God fully and were better cared for than they had ever been while I was with them. I returned with about one dollar in my pocket. My wife had fifty dollars in bank. "Faithful is He who calleth you, who also will do it."

Brother Pike very kindly wrote the following notice of my trip in the "Way of Faith" when I started: "We take pleasure in publishing the personal letter of Brother Bartleman, who is following what he believes to be divine guidance, in his trip around the world. We do not know of anyone whose ministry is more needed, and will be more helpful in the present stage of the Pentecostal movement, than our dear Brother Bartleman." —J. M. Pike. I appreciated greatly this note of confidence. Also the following by the editor of the "Latter Rain:" "Brother Bartleman spent a few days with us just before he sailed for England. Our Brother is filling a very important place in this movement, in Bible teaching, and sober counsel, which is as ballast to a ship in storm. Let us follow this self-sacrificing servant of God with our prayers and support, as he goes out into the regions beyond."

Brother Albert Norton wrote for the "Way of Faith," from Dhond, India: "We were privileged last month to have a visit at Dhond from Brother Daniel Aurey, and Brother Frank Bartleman. Both of these beloved servants of Christ, like Barnabas, were "full of faith and the Holy Ghost," and they received a warm welcome both at Dhond and at Kedgaon (Ramabai's). Our only regret was that they could not stop longer in India." —Albert Norton. Brother Aurey and myself arrived in India on different vessels, providentially, at the same time.

Brother Pike wrote in "Way of Faith," at my home coming, as follows: "Our readers will join us in humble and hearty thanks to God for keeping our dear brother on land and sea, in storm and calm, amid friends and foes, unwholesome surroundings and uncomfortable lodgings. Amid all he has been kept in health, and we believe has fulfilled the mission which was accomplished, under divine direction. The results of that mission will only be known when the books are opened and the record read. Money to meet every necessity as it was presented was on hand, sent in direct answer to prayer, without any personal solicitation." —J. M. Pike. I feel personally I can never be too grateful to God for the facts contained in this statement.

Pastor Alex. Boddy, of Sunderland, England, very kindly wrote the following in "Confidence:" "Brother Bartleman is known to many through his recent journey around the world, and also through his writings. His life is a "life of faith," and on that round the world journey all his needs were wonderfully supplied. He never, however, mentions his circumstances, and we should uphold him in prayer. He is always about his Father's business, without a thought as to self." —Alex. Boddy.

While I am not able to describe my world trip here (the reader can secure this from me, in separate booklet, at any time), yet I feel to repeat a few statements published from my pen in the "Way of Faith," upon my safe home arrival, as follows: "I am so glad I was 'not disobedient to the heavenly vision.' Before I started I received a number of communications, both encouraging and discouraging. Some prophesied blessing, others disaster. Having settled it in my heart however that it was God's call, and not my own imagination and desire, I could do no other than go. If the Lord did not take me around I do not know who did. I did not pull any wires, no individual or Assembly pledged my traveling expenses, and I did not pledge or commit myself to any man or party. I knew that God was sending, and I trusted Him fully to take me through. Physically I had reason to believe, in the natural, that I might not live to get half way around. But I was not going in the natural.

"In a wonderful way the Lord preserved me from sickness. I passed through cholera, plague, and smallpox districts and exposure, and through fever sections at the most deadly time of the year. But the Lord preserved me. I came home weighing ten pounds heavier than I had weighed for years. My family had been kept in fair health during my absence, and with plenty for their temporal needs. I never asked for a penny nor a collection. All was given me voluntarily. I only received fifty dollars from America after leaving her shores. In Palestine, India and China, help came from the most unexpected and unlikely sources. God proved He could provide abroad as well as at home. I reached China with only ten dollars. No money came from America to me there. I visited England, Scotland, Ireland, Wales, Holland, Germany,

Belgium, France, Switzerland, Italy, Egypt, Palestine, Ceylon, India, China and Japan, touching at Honolulu on the way home. Reached home February 25, 1911."

CHAPTER 8

~

Brother Durham in Los Angeles

Just about one week before I arrived home Brother Durham began meetings at old Azusa Mission. He was sent of the Lord from Chicago with a message for the Pentecostal saints in Los Angeles. He was first refused a hearing at Upper Room Mission, so he went to Azusa street. Brother Seymour was absent in the east. He started meetings and the saints flocked back to the old place and filled it again with the high praises of God. This was what the Lord witnessed to three of us while in prayer, more than a year before. I had gotten back just in time to see it. God had gathered many of the old Azusa workers back, from many parts of the world, to Los Angeles again evidently for this. It was called by many the second shower of the Latter Rain. On Sunday the place was crowded and five hundred were turned away. The people would not leave their seats between meetings for fear of losing them.

With this the bottom dropped out of Upper Room Mission over night. The leader had abused his privilege, and also the saints. He had failed God in other ways also. The Lord can spare any man or mission if He is obliged to. We cannot persistently abuse our privilege, destroy the prophets of God, and hope to finally get away with it. Great was the fall of Upper Room Mission. The leader had at one time been much used- of God. But God had another place, man, and message ready. He never deserts His true flock. The "cloud" moved on, and the saints with it.

The fire began to fall at old Azusa as at the beginning. I attended these meetings with great interest and joy. The Lord also blessed me much at Eighth and Maple, which was still running. At Lake Avenue, Pasadena, the little Methodist Church where God had wrought in 1905 so blessedly, had now for some time been turned over to the Pentecostal saints. They still occupy it at this writing.

We moved to Long Beach soon after my return, my family needing a change from Gless street very badly. We were invited to occupy a nice Rest Cottage Home, at 323 Short street, ready furnished, quite near the beach. This was a great treat. We had not even dared ask the Lord for so much. But He was so good to us. May 2, I went to Azusa street, after noon, as usual. But to our surprise we found the doors all locked, with chain and padlock. Brother Seymour had hastened back from the east and with his trustees decided to lock Brother Durham out. But they locked God and the saints out also, from the old cradle of power. It was Durham's message they objected to.

I secured Kohler Street Mission temporarily, and the "cloud" moved with us. Rather, it led us there. In a few days Brother Durham rented a large building at the corner of Seventh and Los Angeles streets. A thousand people attended the meetings here on Sundays. We had an ordinary congregation of four hundred week nights. Here the "cloud" rested. God's glory filled the place. "Azusa" became deserted. The Lord was with Brother Durham in great power. **God sets His seal especially on present truth to be established.** He preached a gospel of salvation by faith. He was used mightily to draw anew a clear line of demarcation between salvation by works and faith, between law and grace. This had become very much needed, even among the Pentecostal people. And it is certain that such a revelation and reformation is needed in the churches today almost as badly as in Luther's day. We have largely a Romanized Protestantism.

"Learn from me," said Luther, "how difficult a thing it is to throw off errors confirmed by the example of all the world, and which, through long habit, have become a second nature to us." But a multitude of souls accepted the message Brother Durham brought with joy. "Men were astonished that they had not earlier acknowledged truths that appeared so evident in Luther's mouth," says the historian, D'Aubigne. And so with Durham's message. But it received great opposition also. Some abused the message, as they do every message sent of God, going to the extreme of declaring that because the work of redemption was fully accomplished on the cross it was of necessity finished in us also, the moment we believed. This was a great error, and hindered the message and work considerably. Man always adds to the message God has given. This is Satan's chief way to discredit and destroy it. Both Luther and Wesley had the same difficulties to contend with. And so has every God given revival. Men are creatures of extremes. The message generally suffers more from its friends than from its foes. We have this treasure in "earthen vessels." The truth can always be abused. Some even went so far as to fight the principle of holiness itself, pretending to justify themselves by Durham's message. But they had either misunderstood it, or more likely seized a pretended opportunity to fight the principle that their own hearts refused to yield to, and thus abused the message God had brought them.

The owner of the Rest Home in Long Beach decided to sell it, so we were obliged to move. We returned July 1 to the Pentecostal Home, at 786 Winona avenue, Pasadena, where we had lived before I went to Hawaii in 1909. We should have moved one month earlier, but a party occupied the house and would not move, though God called them to Sacramento. Refusing to obey God they kept us out, and caused much suffering all around. They confessed their wrong later. Thus they missed the mind of the Lord for themselves, got out of divine order, and suffered much, besides causing great suffering to others. The party owning the beach home insisted on our vacating, but we had no place to go. God wanted us in the Home in Pasadena. We never know how much we are causing others to suffer when we are failing God ourselves. The Lord had blessed our stay in Long Beach. But now He wanted us in Pasadena.

I had a terrible attack of hemmorhoids, and was prostrated for days, suffering awful things, soon after arriving in Pasadena. Through earnest prayer the Lord delivered. My nervous system suffered greatly. It was an awful strain on the nerve centers, and the brain. Little John was taken with a terrible attack of convulsions also. The devil tried to kill him. Through prayer his life was spared. Many times the devil has come to me and actually tried to bargain with me. He has promised me if I would not press him quite so hard he would let me off easier. But God forbid that I should ever bargain thus with him.

1911 was a wonderful year in Los Angeles. The battle was clearly between works and faith, between law and grace. Much of the old time power and glory of the Azusa Mission days returned to us. I had much liberty and joy in Brother Durham's mission, especially in the beginning. God had prepared me beforehand peculiarly for the message. I had been brought completely to the end of self-dependence. Works had no further place with me in meriting salvation. "For we are His workmanship, created in Christ Jesus, unto good works." —Eph. 2:10. We were called to humility again that the power of God might rest upon us.

So determined was I to take no chances of self surviving in my life that I burned at this time no less than five hundred personal letters that I had received in the early Azusa days, from leading church workers, preachers and teachers, all over the world, inquiring anxiously about the revival that was then in our midst. Some of these inquirers were in very high positions officially. They had read my reports of the revival in various papers. But I was afraid these letters might some day prove a temptation to me to imagine that I had been a person of some importance. Many of these inquirers begged an interest in my prayers. I almost wish at times that I had kept these letters. They would have been of much interest now as historical evidence to the widespread influence of the revival. No doubt the Lord could have kept me humble without this sacrifice, but I determined to take no chances. So deep and genuine was the work begun again in our hearts in Brother Durham's day.

We feared nothing more in those days than to seek our own glory, or that the Pentecostal experience should become a matter of past history. In fact we hoped and believed that the revival would last without cessation until Jesus should come, which it doubtless would, and should, if men would not fail God. But we drift back continually into the old, backslidden, ecclesiastical conceptions, forms and ceremonies. Thus history sadly ever repeats itself. Now we must work up an annual revival. We go to church on Sundays, etc., etc., just "like the nations (churches) 'round about us." But in the beginning it was not so. In the early Azusa days you could hardly keep the saints off their knees.

Whenever two saints met they invariably went to prayer. Today we can hardly be dragged to prayer. Some make as much fuss about it as the old camel does in the east in kneeling to receive his load. He fusses, and bites, and groans, before the driver can bring him down. I am glad I did not destroy my diary, however, nor the articles I wrote all through those early Pentecostal days, with reports of meetings, experiences in different parts of the world, etc. I have preserved between five and six hundred separate, printed articles, besides more than one hundred different tracts written and published in the same connection. From these I have been able to draw a tremendous amount of most reliable information for the present book. Had I destroyed these the book would probably have never been written. In all my writings for at least twenty-five years I have labored for the unity of the body of Christ. They are full of the sentiment of John 17:21. I have also plead for reality from the beginning. My first article was titled, "Live the Life." My second one, "Salvation vs. Imitation."

The Lord gave us a little private school in Pasadena for our children. We had dreaded to throw them in among public school influences. Sister Anna Palmer, a precious Pentecostal sister, came to live with us and to teach them. She was a woman of most sterling character, and absolutely self-sacrificing spirit. She was also a woman of special ability. It was purely a labor of love on her part, for the Lord. Some of the neighboring children availed themselves of this opportunity also. We were very grateful for this, God's special mercy.

I had a powerful manifestation of the Spirit about this time at Lake Avenue Mission, Pasadena. The power of God came on me one Sunday morning, as I sat in my chair in the meeting. The Lord had given me a tremendous message on the way to the meeting. Brother Ansel Post had the floor and was commenting on the Word. What he was saying was good, but without special anointing. Suddenly the Lord anointed me to give my message. I hesitated, as Brother Post had the floor. The Spirit ran through me like a sword thrust and I was lifted from my chair. I ran across the floor shouting at the top of my voice, but sat down again. I did not want to interfere with the one speaking. The message was almost consuming me. I had already hesitated too long. God wanted it delivered then. The Spirit struck me again and nearly threw me off my chair. Then I knew I must obey God. I got up and spoke to Brother Post and he graciously gave way to me. I delivered the message with great anointing. How many times I have failed God by not obeying Him under similar circumstances. It seemed this time as though God would kill me if I did not obey Him. We fear to grieve men more than we do Him. It requires much grace to obey God under such circumstances.

I had much ministry and blessing in Brother Durham's mission during this summer. I also wrote and published a little booklet, entitled "A Prophetic Chart," which the Lord gave me. Three thousand of them cost me thirty-five dollars. He provided the means. We moved from Winona avenue to Altadena in September. Our home was on Pine street. Here we opened a little day school, with Miss Palmer for teacher. Other children came from the neighborhood. We saw some very hard financial pressure here. One sister gave me twenty-five dollars, in answer to most earnest prayer. I began to have a strong desire to get out into the active work of the Lord again.

Taking a little trip to San Diego, I preached nine times, with much blessing. I then took a trip, by water, to Oakland, where I held some meetings, with considerable blessing and profit. From there I went to Stockton, where I preached twice, but found a hard field. The spirit was not deep. Returning home I worked in Brother Durham's mission again.

The opposition against Brother Durham was tremendous and he was finally tempted to strike back. This I felt was not the Spirit of Christ, though he had tremendous provocation. Possibly few have been able to stand successfully such a test. I left the platform finally, not willing to stand for a spirit of retaliation. I felt I must keep clear of carnal strife and controversy. But the Lord had wonderfully used dear Brother Durham. He was sent of God to Los Angeles. Possibly his work was done. For him to have remained much longer might have destroyed his victory. His word was coming to be almost law in the Pentecostal missions, even as far as the Atlantic Coast. The paper he instituted in connection with his work began to take on especially the nature of a carnal controversy, fighting the old "second work of grace" theory. This spirit the Lord showed me He was about to stop. Too much power is unsafe for any one man also.

Brother Durham wrote the following observations on the work some time before he died, which are of such vital importance we feel led to reproduce them, as follows: "A great crisis is now on. Men do not see the plan of God in the present Pentecostal movement. Such a complete revolution is necessary that it staggers them. They are unwilling to see that which they have labored so hard to build up, thrown down; but before God's plans can be carried out, man's plans must be set aside. They fail to see that God, having set aside all the plans of man, is beginning to work after His own plan. God is revealing His real plan to so many that they will never consent to having the present work turned into a sect. God's people are simply not going to be led into the snare of human organization again.

~ 214 ~

"God has poured out His Spirit again that Jesus may be glorified. All past movements have resulted in the promotion to positions of honor of one or more men. The present movement will honor and exalt Jesus Christ. The Holy Spirit always exalts Jesus, and His precious blood. As He is exalted, and faithfully preached, God is restoring the old time power. But it is not all restored yet. Not seeing the plan of God, men have not met the conditions, and therefore have not received all God has for them by a great deal. Many have run ahead of God."

Shortly after God filled me, His Spirit rested mightily upon me one morning, and He said to me: "If you were only small enough I could do anything with you." A great desire to be little, yea, to be nothing, came into my heart. But it has been, oh, so hard to keep low enough for Him to really work through me. And He only really uses me when I am little in my own eyes, and really humble at His feet. When I feel that I must do something, He always lets me fail. But when I stay at His feet, and feel that I am nothing, and that He is all, and so just trust Him, He does His work in such a beautiful way that it is wonderful to me.

"God is not trying to build up something else, or to do something for men that will make them great and mighty, but rather to bring all men to naught, and do the work through the power of the Holy Ghost. The call of God to His people now is to humble themselves; to recognize their weakness and lack of power, to get down before Him, and wait till His power is restored. The great question is, will men see the plan of God, and yield to it? Will men get down in humility at Jesus' feet, and pray and wait till He restores His full, Pentecostal power? Or will they continue to run ahead of Him, and fail in the end?

"Let God's people everywhere see His plan, and begin to seek in deep, true humility. Then He will reveal Himself, and. His plan, to them. One man with the real power of God upon him can do more than a thousand who go on their own account. Only those who are true and loyal to God, and His present day message, will share in this great victory. The company who really humble themselves, and stand the test, God will use to do His work." —Wm. H. Durham. The fact is when a man gets to the place where he really loves obscurity, where he does not care to preach, and where he would rather sit in the back seat than on the platform, then God can lift him up and use him, and not very much before.

The old Upper Room, 327½ South Spring street, was opened up again about this time, under the leadership of Brother Warren Fisher, Brother Manley and Brother Allen. I delivered a message there one Sunday and two received the "baptism." God wonderfully anointed me. The presence of the Lord was very near. I had asked Him for a witness. So I now shifted my ministry to the Upper Room Mission. Conditions seemed to be changing at Brother Durham's mission. After I left his platform he seemed to mistrust me. Perhaps he thought I would work against him. I spoke many times now the Upper Room Mission where the Lord greatly blessed me. Brother Durham soon after this went to Chicago to hold a convention. It was in the winter and he contracted a cold there, from the effects of which he soon after died, after having returned to Los Angeles. He was wonderfully used in Chicago.

By this time the Lord was speaking loudly to me about getting out into the field again, with my family. I felt strongly drawn to Europe. I had had a conviction of this when passing through Europe in 1910. The time had come. The Lord began to touch hearts in a marked way on our behalf, to this end, although nearly all of our financial help, as it always had, peculiarly, before, came from outside of Los Angeles. A brother in Stockton, and a sister (not Pentecostal), in Pasadena, furnished our fares to Denver, our first stop. God did not allow any mission or party as such to send us forth. And perhaps it was better so. Today you are all right. Tomorrow you may be standing on your head with them. So it is better at least to look to God. Our poor missionaries on the foreign field seldom know where they stand in relation to most of the missions. Before the next letter can pass between them the whole doctrinal situation may be changed, or the society have been totally dissolved for that matter. They need our sympathy and our prayers. When will God's people become "one flock," with "one Shepherd," Jesus, as He has promised? It is surely time to pray as Jesus prayed, "that they all may be one; that the world may believe." —John 17:21.

We left Los Angeles, after sacrificing our little all of household goods, as we had so often done before, and started to work our way across the continent once more, this time, as we believed, enroute for Europe. We had just enough money to take us to Denver. But the account of our 'Two Years Mission Work in Europe, Just Before the World-War, 1912 to 1914," with labors in England, Scotland, Wales, Holland, Switzerland, France, Germany, Norway, Sweden, Finland, and old Russia itself, where I had to preach in secret, although almost under the Czar's nose; with a lively account of the first few weeks of the Great World War, before we got out of Europe, and which finally drove us back to America, through the war zone, must be secured in a separate booklet, already published, price 30¢. We did not want to return to America so soon, but were obliged to, in safety to the family. Besides, the whole effort of the nations now became one of filling their people's hearts with hate and murder. There seemed no place for the spirit of the Gospel. The Sermon on the Mount has nothing whatever in common with the tenets of the "god of war." You are expected to do all you can to hate, curse, or kill the enemy in war-time, certainly not to love him. Let others do this, however, if they will; but as for me, the Gospel is just the same in peace or war. "Jesus Christ the same, yesterday, today, and forever."

Los Angeles, Calif., April, 1925.

CHAPTER 9

◦◦◦

Sparks from the Anvil

"The Fathers must be explained, interpreted, according to Scripture, and not Scripture according to the Fathers. How often has not Jerome, Augustine, and Ambrose been mistaken! How often their opinions are different, and thy retract their errors!" —Melancthon

"The highest degree of wisdom attained by ambitious minds, or by souls thirsting with the desire for perfection, has been to despair of themselves." —D'Aubigne.

"God, who prepares His work through ages, accomplishes it by the weakest instruments, when His time is come, that the work may be seen to be of God and not of man. To effect great results by imperceptible means such is the law of God." —D'Aubigne.

"It is a sair thing to the flesh for a man to have a little mair light than his brethren." A Scotch saying. They will make him smart for it.

The early church put God first, self last. We have self first, God last. This was the secret of the early church's power. The church is a backslider. But we are coming around the circle. She is to be fully restored. The Spirit is lifted from her, as in Ezekiel's vision. Her ministers need to "weep between the porch and the altar." The "carcasses" of the old crowd may have to "fall in the wilderness" today. We are too hard-hearted. Oh, to be a Joshua, or a Caleb!

There are two errors to be avoided. Dictatorship, and lawlessness. Unorganized missions frequently have a tighter ring of fellowship than those organized. Sects generally begin with an honest effort to preserve and restore some long lost truth. They end in division. History repeats itself. No religious body has ever recovered itself after its "first love" was lost.

Every wrong influence in Christian profession makes the way just that much harder for the whole body of Christ. Each individual must be judged also on his own merits, apart from the particular party that he runs with.

The "tongues" were the "sign," the "burning bush," that God used to attract the attention of the people to the Pentecostal outpouring, as he had used "healing," etc., in previous outpourings. What particular "sign" will accompany the next outpouring?

Philosophical reasonings, intellectual speculations, etc., are rampant and the contagion of the hour, actuated by demon forces, to sweep us from the basis of a childlike faith in God, salvation through the blood. Many are in a mental maze, beguiled by the "serpent," like Eve. This is a terrible universe to be lost in.

To be like Jesus, is the standard that God has set us. **Be as much in earnest as God is.** If Heaven is real we should live like it. This will produce "Pentecost." The human spirit too often predominates, while love and humility are clothed in rags and sit by the wayside begging. The gentle Jesus is run over again and again and knocked down in the meetings. Sin and the "flesh" will kill any "Pentecost." The doctor looks at the tongue first thing. Have you been speaking evil? That denotes a bad heart. Every radical movement for God has ultimately failed on the test of love. The Philadelphia church ("brotherly love"), had the "open door." —Rev. 3.

If they had been "digging," going down, at Babel, instead of going up, God might have spared them. Israel sinned by asking an earthly king, and dividing the nation. We reject the Spirit rule, and divide the "body." "If thou take the precious from the vile, thou shalt be as My mouth." —Jer. 15:19. Better grieve all men than God. **The very truths that gave birth to the Pentecostal movement are today generally rejected as too strong.** But if Israel followed the pillar of fire and cloud so carefully, how much more should we the Holy Ghost. Every work of God so far has been sidetracked, or fallen short of its real object and purpose. Hence we have needed "new lumps" continually. Party spirit, and temporal interest, self, is the difficulty.

We have too much Chinese Joss, and Dance Hall Jazz music. Charles G. Finney, the mighty evangelist, discouraged even too much good singing. It kills conviction. We spend too much steam on our whistle. Pentecost means "fifty." Some of ours is "fifty-fifty."

Millions are shut up in fixed systems of finality, both doctrinally and experimentally. They are bound, and frightened to move out with God in his great, green pasture. Tied to a stake, the pasture is all gone. The stream is moving beneath them, but they fear to let go the bank, separate from past attachments, and trust themselves to the current of God's onward move in restoration of truth once lost. Heathen, not indoctrinated, realize God's sovereignty of operation. They get the most.

Both Jonah and Balaam had the "gift of prophecy," but were largely graceless men. We need holiness of heart. It is a vital error to substitute light for heat. "Knowledge puffeth up, but charity (love), edifieth." Read 1 Cor. 13, once more. Be not drawn away from "the simplicity that is in Christ." Faith gets the most, love works the most, humility keeps the most. God's vision comes to humble men. He who seeks to make foot-prints and do sublime things is a failure. A self-conscious poser is a loser. Let self intrude and the whole is spoiled. Excellency is proportioned to the oblivion of self. A fisher for compliments has lost God. Self-consciousness must go. We are too conscious of the other fellow also. We need God-consciousness.

Humility, not infallibility, becomes fallen creatures. Water seeks the low places. Infallibility is the apex of Satan's proposition to man. The deepest repentance and humility, our own frailty and weakness, must be realized before we can know God's strength. Receding guns vanish out of sight after firing. And so must we, for safety. We need to be "broken."

Zealous religionists care only for the triumph of their particular doctrine or party. Any one can have a standing and prestige if they will but work for some party's selfish interest. To stand for principle alone is another thing. Such are little understood. A selfish person can never understand unselfishness.

Most people need to carry heavy to keep steady. Waiting is God's common instrument of providential discipline. He tries acceptable men in the furnace of affliction. Most great men accomplish their life work in a short time. It burns them up. No man creates his own times. The times create the man.

The devil has no conscience, the "flesh" has no sense. Then why expect them to behave themselves in meeting? We should act and speak as in the immediate, conscious presence of God. Settle all differences before His throne also. Protect others' good name and they will speak well of you. Our influence, for good or evil, sets waves in motion only to break on the shores of eternity. A little push, just at the right time, may hurl a soul to hell, or lift it to Heaven.

Priest-craft is passing away. Men think for themselves today, not one man for thousands. The Holy Spirit will not resign His authority to any man or party. We have too much dogmatic controversy. To analyze Christ is to destroy Him. Terms mean little, except for conscious realization.

The human soul is naturally lazy toward God. All the weakness of humanity is shown up under the "Pentecostal baptism." We have but one life, one chance. It will pass quickly. Are our spiritual stocks inflated? Better take account.

"Seven years of plenty," in the beginning of the Pentecostal outpouring. "Seven years of famine," with the advent of the World War. We prophesied of this in the beginning. We also saw that the churches would largely go into it. This brought a hardening over the whole religious situation. What next? Luther looked for the "end of the world" in his day.

"Know no man after the flesh." What would this do to most of our meetings, which have become a babel of confusion and over-developed, fleshly sociability? They are as hard to sink into God in as the Dead Sea. The waves of human enthusiasm and zeal have no rest. In "Azusa" days when two saints met they invariably went to prayer. We could scarcely keep off our knees. In those days we had to dig the preachers out of the sawdust. Today we cannot keep them off the platform. They make a fearful howl if not invited.

Jesus in town would stop the traffic. He would stand in a class by Himself. But we need men with His character and spirit to handle the situation. Few men are big enough to deal with the difficulties, questions, and the people in the missions, successfully. We need more wisdom, patience, humility, love, everything. What would Jesus do? We need deliverance from strife and confusion, a deeper consecration and death to self. Human zeal and enthusiasm, the spirit of joking and lightness, in the preacher or Assembly, must result in ruin. If we have lost our "pilgrim and stranger" role we are not Bible Christians. Cares of life, deceitfulness of riches, covetousness, etc., are the "canker-worms." Most Christians get their "oil" at the gasoline station.

The organized church has largely proven a tremendous framework of form and ceremony, built up against God. The Spirit had no right of way. They would offer violence if pressed by the claims of Jesus, as in His day. Are we not drifting also? Large churches, popular evangelism, sensational advertising, etc., etc. "One man" meetings, order of services announced beforehand. Is this "Pentecostal?" We have got to leave room for God somewhere. We need not be lawless either. We have gotten the Ark on a "new cart" again. God smote Uzzah for this mistake, and David left it by the way. When they put it on the "priests' shoulders" again all went well. —2 Sam'l 6. We advertise "miracles," wonderful preachers, etc., and have the crowds following the bill-board "signs," to the next big meeting. But are the "signs following?" Men love the spectacular. What we do not understand is "wonderful."

God's fire falls on sacrifice, as in Elijah's case. The greater the sacrifice, consecration, the more fire. But Ananias and Sapphira are in the mission work today. They are striking the Peters dead, with their money and influence. The man who is paying the full price in consecration has very little voice in the meetings. Then multitudes are evidently serving the Lord for what they can get out of it, in selfish blessing, etc. There are plenty of "rice Christians" in America. A young man will sacrifice everything, even life if need be, for the girl he loves. Do we really love the Lord?

The Holy Ghost was given to witness of the "resurrection," not to help propagate every little fellow's pet notion and theory. The truth discovers itself to, and makes its dwelling with, the humble. The "baptism" is only a beginning, not the end all. He is to "guide us into all truth." The early church started out with it. We are coming back to the beginning, ready to start, from the church's fall.

The Christian life is a "travail." We are on probation until finally delivered. "He must increase, but I must decrease." Luther's translation of the New Testament, the greatest work of his age, did not bear his name. It read, "The New Testament-German-Wittemberg." Here was self-abnegation. These are times of general sacrilege and peculiar presumption. Beware of undue familiarity with God. "Fools rush in where angels fear to tread." Let the lid stay on the Ark. —1 Sam'l 6:19. Daniel, and John the Revelator, fell on their faces when they met God.

A woman after child-birth is subdued, but has a joy that no other knows. The father does the shouting. Demonstration is not necessarily deep joy. Crude spirits trample the gentle spirit of Jesus under foot. Possibly ninety per cent of religious demonstration since the early church's fall has been human. Note the continuous warring of sects, strife of creeds, contention, and even inquisition.

Keep free from party spirit if you would have a clear vision, and speak the truth at all times, without fear or favor. Preach not to please a "party," but to raise a standard. Most movements go 'round a circle. They wear a rut so deep they cannot see out. God has just one "issue." That is "Jesus."

We have too much human manipulation and wizardry. Like the Church of England we must get up, sit down, now do this, now that. Where does "Pentecost" come in at? How can we follow both the Lord and the leader? "No man can serve two masters." Suppose we are in the spirit of prayer? Some leaders like control of their congregations completely. They change the order of service at their own sweet will. We do not believe in lawlessness, but the Spirit must surely have some control. A certain amount of government is necessary at times. But we speak of the abuse of it.

God gathered a lot of seasoned saints together at "Azusa" in the beginning. They were subdued and purified through months of prayer, and years of experience with God. We live in a light, jazzy age, since the war. They refuse the fires of purifying, holiness of heart. We have an atmosphere of confusion. There is too much "professional" work, railroading seekers through, like a "quack" doctor's office. This produces a "fake" Pentecost, with spurious "tongues." The "singing in the Spirit" is also imitated. Men have learned to do these things without the Spirit, and suggest them to others for their imitation. We have even heard leaders call for any demonstration they wanted from the people. What would Peter say to such a demonstration? Many have promised an elephant, but brought forth a mouse. But these are only backslidden substitutions.

Old parties, who are found steeped in bitter, sectional, factional positions, can never be used of God for the next move of the Spirit. History repeats itself. They are in no condition. It requires a "new lump," always. God's people are free-born. Only he who has been in the "mount," has seen the heavenly vision, and received the spirit of obedience, can overleap the chasms, and climb the mountains of doubt and fear to victory. We need men "full of faith and of the Holy Ghost," to lead the people to victory.

Let us appreciate our blood-bought liberty in the Holy Ghost. The early church lost this, and slid into the "dark ages," through compromise with temporal and ecclesiastical abuse and power. We are being tested today on the very same lines. History repeats itself. We are bound for the "dark ages" as a people, if we fail to be warned. Be not entangled again in a yoke of bondage."

Organized effort is proper and exactly as it should be. But party spirit is unchristian and essentially damning. To glory in denominationalism is for the church to glory in its shame.

CHAPTER 10

A Plea for Unity

Dr. Philip Schaff, the well known scholar, has happily declared: "The divisions of Christendom will be overruled at last for a deeper and richer harmony, of which Christ is the key-note. In Him and by Him all problems of theology and history will be solved. In the best case a human creed is only an approximate and relatively correct expression of revealed truth, and may be improved by the progressive knowledge of the church, while the Bible remains perfect and infallible. Any higher view of the authority of creeds is unprotestant and essentially Romanizing."

The editor of "The Friend of Russia" writes: "God's people can never get together on human creeds and disciplines. They are too narrow and changeable. We have a foundation that is broad enough to hold all. Christ Himself is this foundation. In Christ, all God's people are one, irrespective of race, color, social standing, or creed."

A certain preacher of standing, in a prominent church outside the Pentecostal ranks, addressing the "baptized" saints not long ago, said: "As we look upon the church divided, upon the sect-ridden multitude, none of whom can see alike, how our tried souls cry out for that original love, and we will never win the world on any other plane. It was said of the early Christians, by the beholding heathen, 'Behold how these Christians love one another!' While we are breaking up into sects, creeds, isms, and doctrines, our love is dying, our churches will be empty, and our people lost. Your beautiful Pentecostal work, so full of promise, where God has designed to come in and fill souls and wonderfully baptize them in the Holy Ghost, is broken and peeled and ruined for lack of love." Is not this a terrible indictment?

Eric Booth-Clibborn, one of our own people, who recently died in Africa, wrote: "Before the terrible agony of Gethsemane, our blessed Savior prayed earnestly that His disciples might be one even as He was one with the Father. As long as the church was contending with the onrushing forces of heathenism, it was kept pure and united, but as soon as it lost out in this conflict, the warfare instead of being with the outside forces of evil, was now within the church's walls. There arose terrible controversies. The Ecumenical Councils called for the purpose of peace and unity, brought nothing but dishonor and disgrace on the name of Christ, by the hatred and dissension manifested there. I have been in many places where 'Pentecost' had 'gone to seed.' They had been busy setting the other fellow right, and advancing some pet theme or doctrine. As to proving the other fellow to be wrong, this will take care of itself as we get on the forward march."

Someone has said: "On the day of battle one and the same feeling animates every bosom; after the victory they become divided." And this is only too sadly true of God's people.

Shortly after the World War started the Kaiser of Germany had a medal struck, with the following inscriptions on either side: "I know no parties more, I know only Germans."

"The King called, and they all came." And should not the church be at least as wise?

John Wesley wrote the following: "I am sick of opinions. Give me a humble, gentle, lover of God and man, a man full of mercy and good fruits; without partiality or hypocrisy. Let my soul be with such Christians, wheresoever they are and whatsoever opinion they are of. Whosoever doeth the will of my Father, the same is my brother."

In an article against bigotry Wesley wrote: "Bigotry is too strong an attachment to, or fondness for, our own party or opinion. How unwilling men are to allow anything good in those who do not in all things agree with themselves. We must not narrow the cause of God to our own party, but rejoice in goodness, wherever it appears."

Wesley writes again: "May we not all be of one heart, though not of one opinion? Without doubt we may. There was a time when all Christians were of one mind, as well as of one heart; so great grace was upon them all, **when they were first filled with the Holy Ghost.** But no animosities are so deep and irreconcilable as those that spring from disagreement in religion." What a terrible statement, yet how true.

The recovery of the church to unity again, as at the beginning, has been the fond dream of many of the noblest minds in Christendom. Melancthon's famous maxim was: "In essentials unity, in doubtful points liberty, in all things charity." Melancthon labored for the unity of the body of Christ unceasingly in his day. We hear some saints say this can never be. Then we shall have to reject the last prayer of our Savior, in John 17. Possibly few would care to confess that the Lord could not restore them to this right Christian spirit. Then if myself, why not the other fellow? Am I of so much more hopeful fibre than he?

As a matter of history even the Greek Orthodox Church has looked forward hopefully since the Seventh Ecumenical Council, A. D. 787, to a future Eighth one (not yet held), when all the controversies of Christendom will be settled. They know they should be.

We are told that when General Allenby took Jerusalem he did not know what to do with the Church of the Holy Sepulchre. He could not find a real Christian committee to entrust with its care. The Christian sects hate each other so there. There are an even dozen of them worshipping under the same roof. So he was obliged to appoint an old Moslem to make up the timetable for the services of these various sects, and to keep them from actually killing one another in their religious fervor (a thing that often happens there). Under the old regime the Turkish guard kept order. This old Moslem laughingly tells the visitor that he is there to keep the Christians from killing one another. And he tells no lie. Can anyone tell us about how long it ought to take to get this Moslem converted at this rate?

History records of the Crusaders of the Middle Ages, the following: "The pious pilgrims entering humble and barefoot within the walls of Jerusalem, burned the Jews in their Synagogue, and watered with the blood of thousands of the Saracens the places where they came to trace the sacred footsteps of the Prince of Peace." Is it any great wonder the Jews have not been saved? Think of the "pogroms" in Russia, instituted by the Greek Orthodox Church against the Jews. The State Church in Europe, for centuries past, whenever waxing especially zealous, would pledge themselves to plunder the Jews.

Someone has said: "The passions never show themselves more violently than in religious discussion." It is a fact also that in no part of the world have there been more terrible wars than among Christians. Instance the one just past. These things being facts how it behooves us all to see that we have the Spirit of Christ, and not that of religion. Someone has also declared, "Factions are pitiless, and what should excite their compassion, does but inflame their anger." Multitudes seem to really think seriously that "the end justifies the means" in religion.

Luther in his day writes of the spirit of disunity among the various sects and divisions of the Roman Church, as follows: "Priests, monks, and laymen have come to hate each other more than the Christians hate the Turks. Each one is attached to his own sect, and despises all others. The unity and charity of Christ are at an end." So it appeared to Luther.

The historian, D'Aubigne, writing of the Reformation in Switzerland, says: "The Dominicans and Augustines and Capuchins, so long at enmity, were reduced to the necessity of living together (because of poverty); a foretaste of hell for these poor monks."

In the Council where Luther and Zwingle finally met, Zwingle plead with Luther to be reconciled to the Swiss reformers. "Let us confess, said he, our union in all things in which we agree; and as for the rest let us remember that we are brothers. There will never be peace between the churches if, while we maintain the grand doctrine of faith, we cannot differ on secondary points." Luther was very slow to yield this point, and as a consequence of his uncharitable and violent spirit he fell into a fit of melancholy and despair in which he felt God Himself had forsaken him. And so He doubtless had, for the time. Love is its own avenger, and Luther had violated that very principle. And that is the exact trouble with a multitude of preachers who suffer at times great depression of spirit. It is the law of retribution, rebounding on their own heads. When Zwingle and

Luther finally did get together they were astonished to find in how many things they agreed. How much better it would be today if we would seek to find how many things we agree in, instead of how many we can differ in.

H. L. Hastings has written as follows: "It seems to have been a favorite device of the devil for ages to nickname, and thus separate and persecute the people of God, for whose unity the Savior so earnestly prayed." John Bunyan was very crude. He wrote as follows: "Since you desire to know by what name I wish to be called, I desire, if God should count me worthy, to be called a Christian, a believer, or any other name sanctioned by the Holy Ghost. But as for those factious titles, such as Anabaptists, etc., I believe they came neither from Jerusalem nor Antioch, but rather from hell and Babylon, for they naturally tend to divisions, and ye may know them by their fruits."

Hastings writes further, of conditions shortly after the early church's downfall: "In those old days, when men whose kingdom was 'of this world,' had assumed authority over the flock of God, and had established organizations in which politics was more potent than piety, and where faith instead of coming by hearing, and hearing by the word of God, was settled by the decisions of councils and the decrees of despots, etc."

Hastings writes of James Murdoch, author of the Syriac translation of the New Testament, as follows: "With a well-balanced mind, resisting all tendencies to extremes, a wise sagacity to detect eternal principles, as distinguished from temporary forms of expression, with boldness to cast aside traditional fetters, and a breadth of view which comprehended a subject in all its bearings, his devotion to truth and righteousness was supreme. Questions of minorities, majorities, and policies, were of little account in his eyes."

It is said of Fryth, one of the early reformers: "Instead of propagating his particular opinions and forming divisions, he clung only to the faith which saves, and advanced the dominion of true unity. This," adds the historian, "is the mark of the great servants of God." We are to "contend earnestly" for the great fundamental saving principles of the Gospel, not each for some little pet theory.

Cranmer, another of the reformers, did not embrace any particular party or age; but possessing a free and philosophical mind, he weighed all opinions in the balance of his judgment, taking the Bible for his standard.

How different another character of those times, of which we have far too many today. It is said of him: "Of a restless disposition, unable to enjoy any repose, always requiring new pursuits, he was a torment to all around him. Confusion was his native element; he seemed born for contention, and when he had no adversaries he fell afoul of his friends."

Someone has recently written as follows: "It is a common thing to read in the daily papers such words as these, 'Only union men need apply.' And it is becoming a common thing to read in the Pentecostal papers: 'Affiliating brethren are invited.' What is the difference, asks this writer. And he answers, 'No difference, except one is a secular union, the other is a religious union.'"

Every fresh division or party in the church gives to the world a contradiction as to the oneness of the body of Christ, and the truthfulness of the Gospel. Multitudes are bowing down and burning incense to a doctrine rather than Christ. The many sects in Christendom are, to say the least, evidence to the world that Christians cannot get along together. Written creeds only serve to publish the fact that we cannot understand the Word of God alike, and get together on it. Is the Word of God, then, so hard to understand? They who establish a fixed creed bar the way to further progress.

It is said of the mighty evangelist, Charles G. Finney, that he "forged his theology on the anvil of prayer, in his own heart." He was not bound by the systems of his day.

The Spirit is laboring for the unity of believers today, for the "one body," that the prayer of Jesus may be answered, "that they all may be one, that the world may believe." But the saints are ever too ready rather to serve a system or party, to contend for religious, selfish, party interests. God's people are shut up in denominational coops. Like chicks they must get their food only in these, their own coops. "Error always leads to militant exclusion. Truth evermore stoops to wash the saints' feet." One feels even in visiting many Pentecostal missions today that they do not belong there, simply because they have not lined up officially with that particular brand or variety. These things ought not to be. "In one Spirit are we all baptized, into one body." —1 Cor. 12:13. We should be as one family, which we are, at home in God's house anywhere.

We belong to the whole body of Christ both in Heaven and on earth. God's church is one. It is a terrible thing to go about dismembering the "body of Christ." How foolish and wicked the petty difference between Christians will appear in the light of eternity Christ is the "issue." Not some doctrine about him. The Gospel leads to Him. It exalts Christ, not some particular doctrine, etc. To "know Christ" is the alpha and the omega of the Christian faith and practice.

"The church was in the beginning a community of brethren, guided by a few of the brethren." —D'Aubigne. "One is your Master, even Christ; and all ye are brethren." —Matt. 23:8.

We have too much "leadership" spirit. These divide the "body," separate the saints.

We are coming around the circle, from the early church's fall, back to primitive love and unity, in the "one body" of Christ. This is doubtless the church for which Christ is coming, "without spot or wrinkle, or any such thing."

Name Index

Cecil M. Robeck Jr., PhD, is an ordained Assemblies of God minister who has served on the administration and faculty of Fuller Theological Seminary for over forty years. He is currently senior professor of Church History and Ecumenics and special assistant to the president for Ecumenical Relations. He has two academic passions. The first is the Azusa Street Mission and the revival that exploded there in April 1906. The second is working with Christian leaders all over the world on issues related to the unity of Christ's Church.

Darrin Rodgers, M.A., JD, is director of the Flower Pentecostal Heritage Center (Springfield, Missouri), the Pentecostal archives and research center located in the National Leadership and Resource Center of the Assemblies of God. He also serves as editor of *Assemblies of God Heritage* magazine.